Unlocking the Mystery
of
Divine Healing

Tony Myers

EDITED BY: DIANA JAMERSON

PROOFREAD BY: LYNNE SUSZEK

COVER DESIGN BY: AKIRA GRAPHICZ

Scripture quotations marked (KJV) are from the King James Version of the Bible

Scripture quotations marked (NLT) are taken from the Holy Bible, New Living Translation, copyright© 1996, 2004, 2007 by Tyndale House Foundation. Used by permission of Tyndale House Publishers, Inc, Carol Stream, Illinois 60188. All rights reserved

Occasionally Scripture quotations marked (TV), Tony's Version, is put there to show my interpretation, for emphasis. LOL

Brackets [ ] within a verse contain my interpretation, for emphasis.

Published by: Unit 10936, PO Box 6945 London, W1A 6US
kingdomcollectivepublishing@gmail.com

Kingdom
Collective
Publishing

Table of Contents

DEDICATION

This book is first, dedicated to my lovely faith-filled wife, without whom there would be no "Believer in Christ, Tony."

Next, this book is dedicated and blessed for those who are physically ill or paralyzed at the moment. May this book enrich your life, and bring you hope, and healing.

Also this book is dedicated to those who choose to learn how to share the ministry of Christ in all its fullness. God Bless You.

ACKNOWLEDGMENTS

God Bless those who have so richly blessed me. Of course first and foremost Our Heavenly Father, and my King Christ Jesus. Then there is John and Diana Jamerson, who not only continue to play a large role in my books, but also in friendship.

Corey Shroeter, whose friendship continues to bless me and my wife.

Pamela Brown, who doesn't know, what an inspiration she is to me. This woman, inspires and encourages others, without even trying! I am quite blessed to call her a friend. Pam has gone to her heavenly reward, I dearly miss her.

To those that I have ministered to their loved ones and they succumbed to their heavenly reward, I pray that this book will give some comfort that the more we walk in healing, the more of it we will see. The driving force behind me is to see that no one dies from disease. You know who you are, your friendship and support, has been tantamount!

My behind the scenes friend Mama Setta, who's encouraged me relentlessly throughout the years. She has stood behind my wife and I and been such a reliable friend. She's been a grandmother, mother, and sister to me all rolled up into one.

Mark and Lynne Suszek their help polishing this book up, has been amazing. We've just met, but it's as if our friendship has been going on for years.

There are so many people that played a role with this book, that I wish to acknowledge. You all know who you are much love and thank you.

FOREWORD

Unpolished, un-churchy, up-close and personal, that's Tony Myers. In the time I've come to know him, it seems like we've been friends for years. The reason for that is, we know the same Holy Spirit. As we chatted we have found that our revelations on healing line up as if we have studied the same books but no books have been written with this kind of revelation until now. My blog is the closest you can find to this teaching; with Tony's testimony and this book you're about to read, you will convince your heart of the truth and learn how to believe, be healed and stay well.

Tony was healed of paralysis (but mine is a spinal cord injury) and that's where I'm headed. Pursuing my healing, there's no one better to learn from than he who has "been there and got twelve tee shirts!" Tony has arrived in my Promised-Land-Of-The-Healed and after arriving, he has finally done what most people don't do after a miracle; he figured out how in the world he got there and wants to teach you how to use the faith you already have. His miracle gives me the confident expectation I need to see mine manifest!

Tony's very different writing style had me chuckling, nodding and shaking my head, gasping and praising God while he brought me through his story like I was sitting in front of him for hours as we both sipped our coffee. Thank you, Tony, for your fearless and faith-filled directions on how to believe we are well, just like Jesus said.

Lynne Suszek
Author of <u>First Wash The Inside</u>
Christian Blogger of www.lynneshealingroom.com

PREFACE

Grab a cup of coffee, cuddle up with a good book, oh you are, this one! If you haven't read my testimonial book "The Lord Jesus Healed Me", I recommend that you do so. It is that experience that uniquely qualifies me to write this book. I learned about healing from living through it myself, even before I read scripture. No one taught me how to be healed or how to pray for the sick. I started praying for the sick immediately after my healing, wanting nothing more than to share my healing with others. I simply did what had worked for me and commanded their healing.

For approximately a year and a half, I went about praying for the sick and studying scripture on my own, with no outside influences. Each person I prayed for was unique and I noted that while some got healed, some did not. I have seen Jesus' sacrifice for us manifest in some very amazing ways! I have prayed for people in countless places, with varying belief systems; McDonald's, car dealerships, Wal-mart, Little Caesars etc and also, at church services. Then The Holy Spirit seemed to shift who I prayed for and I began getting phone calls, many of these calls were from those who had prayed for others, and got results, yet, they themselves were sick.

There is a number of people who are walking in the power of Holy Spirit, yet sick or dying themselves. Then there is another category of those who believe in healing and have studied the great teachers in this area. Those are the ones that study other people to find their own healing. They have had countless people pray for them with little or no results. They have been led down varying roads with many different perspectives and teachings. I started ministering to these two categories of people while still doing my street ministry.

There are many good ministries with fine teachings that train people to walk in healing and deliverance and there are just as many bad ones. I am personally very tired of seeing people die, especially those who are seeking Truth and do believe in healing. This book is my effort, with revelation from The Holy Spirit, to streamline beliefs in order to lead more people to the healing that Jesus did paid for.

Curry Blake, of John G. Lake Ministries, has the Divine Healing Technician (DHT), which is the best and most comprehensive. The DHT is designed to teach Christians how to walk in healing. This teaching combats many of the traditions of men. I agree with the DHT and love this teaching. Many people are taught how to minister healing this way and numerous people are healed. I do recommend the DHT teachings. I will not be dealing with the traditions of men individually in this book.

Incidentally, Curry Blake and Andrew Wommack are the two best teachers in our day and age. They are the first two teachers I listened to after my year and half of learning on my own. They were confirmation to me that I was heading in the right direction. In fact, they were a huge encouragement the first time listening to them. It was a huge relief to know that there were others that had come to the same conclusions that I had, and that I wasn't entirely off my rocker!

With those two teachers in mind, you will not read anything that contradicts their perspective teachings. You will find however a different perspective. This is more of a supplement to their teachings or perhaps their teachings may be a supplement to mine. We shall see.

The goal of this book is to provide a baseline from which to believe. A truth of how to view healing and how to achieve it for yourself and others. I will also deal with the follies that many people fall into, including both wrong beliefs and the ways we are distracted from truth. Make sure you have a full pot of coffee brewing, an open heart and mind and a willingness to learn!

1 THE CAUSE OF EVIL STUFF

UGH!! I ran out of coffee! Take a five minute break until mine brews!

In order to arrive at the final resolution of a problem, we must properly determine the cause. The problem: disease, illnesses, and all other causes of death; this would include accidents and murder. It is here where many methods of healing err. They cite the cause of these instances as being an individual's action. For instance, if somebody develops diabetes the cause will be related to having eaten the wrong foods. The person is told they opened the door to this disease by the sin of gluttony. Cancer, by the sin of unforgiveness, or some other "open door" of sin. A theology is implied that sickness is caused by an individual's actions and this, my friends, is where we're missing it.

Death, and its causes, is never caused by individual sin. Yes, I agree that it can look that way. If I were to eat too much and cause myself to weigh four hundred pounds, then one might say that I "opened a door" to heart problems, kidney problems etc. That might appear to be truth and the solution would then be to go on a diet. I can agree that there is an aspect of individual cause and effect. A question might arise; "What originally empowered, eating to affect my health?" In the same manner, unforgiveness causes bitterness and bitterness a plethora of health problems. Again, "What is the original cause of empowering bitterness to effect my health?" Then there is genetics or in religious terminology "generational curses", and again we could ask "What caused this to have the power to appear?" Mind you, we are not looking for the individual cause based on an individual

3

action. We are looking for the original reason that empowered the causes of death.

Poison Ivy, for example, when we are looking to stop the plant from spreading, it would be ineffective to go around and just pluck the leaves off. The root is still there and the leaves will grow back. This is what is happening when we try to achieve healing by looking at an individual action as the source. It would be assumed then that for each onset of illness, we must figure out the individual reason/sin as the cause. This is ineffective and completely unneeded. Why is death on planet earth and what is the permanent solution? AHA!, now you get it! The first Adam was the cause; The Second Adam (JESUS!), is the solution!

Wait for it... my next provocative statement is coming! You will agree with me that Jesus is the solution. Sadly, we are taught that we are still waiting for the final resolution before divine health can be attained. We think diseases are normal and go from one life threatening event to the next. This is two-fold, some people don't get healed because they never find the individual cause. In other cases, they do get healed but then at a later time they fall victim to another illness and die. For now, death is inevitable but it should come peacefully or because of Christ's Name (martyrdom). All things considered, death should not come by disease but rather when we have fulfilled our life's calling as purposed by our loving Heavenly Father. The goal of this chapter, is to prove the root cause of disease and that the solution is available now, to all who believe. When Believers of Christ finally put this to rest, then disease will become a non-issue. Disease still exists because of a lie believed and expected.

ROMANS 5: 12-14 (KJV)
Wherefore as by one man sin entered
into the world, and death by sin; and so
death passed upon all men, for that all have
sinned: (For until the law sin was in the world:
but sin is not imputed when there is no law).
Nevertheless death reigned from Adam to Moses,
even over them that had not sinned after the
similitude of Adam's transgression, who is a figure
of him that was to come.

Understand this and submit it to your whole being, even when sin was not accounted towards men, death, and it's causes, reigned. People did not die because of individual sin, they died because they were included in Adam's sin. It was by Adam, not individual sin, that death and the causes of it reigned. From Adam to Moses no one was held accountable for their individual actions, and yet, they died. In fact, with this truth in mind, here is what happens; we pray for someone to get healed and they don't get healed. Then what do we do; we blame that person's hidden sin. That isn't scriptural at all. We may even make them renounce all their past sin, which is so wrong. Often, even after repenting, they still don't get healed. Let's look at another verse.

ROMANS 5:19 (KJV)
For as by one man's disobedience many
were made sinners, so by the obedience of
one shall many be made righteous.

We are made righteous, by Christ, I know we can agree on that. Just as with Jesus, if we are made righteous then death has no hold on us. Therefore the causes of death have no hold on us. Take a deep breath and let this truth sink in. Grab a cup of coffee and remember that I bring this up to show the cause of disease which is the original sin, not individual sin. Therefore, if the cause of disease is the original sin, focusing on individual sin for healing is completely wrong. Along the same lines, if we think we aren't receiving healing because of individual sin, then we're still wrong.

DISCLAIMER: WE ARE TO LIVE SANCTIFIED LIVES. WE ARE TO REPENT. Grace is empowerment to not sin. I am simply bringing truth in order for you to receive your healing. Did Christ take care of the original sin - Yes or No? Of course He did, therefore He took care of the causes of death for those that believe He did! Right now, many of you are thinking of the old covenant, the law of Moses that says otherwise. What about that? Let's take a minute to catch our breath, and drink some coffee. The point I am making, along with the other chapters will all tie together nicely in a pretty little bow.

This should be a one sentence explanation, but it won't be. We aren't under the Law of Moses, nor ever were. Jesus fulfilled the law two thousand years ago (see the Disclaimer, above). This book is about healing. and I will not be going into the long explanation of the difference in the old and new covenant. Simply put, if we position any action of our own as a means to get something, then it becomes the law to you and you are cut off from Christ. If you think you're sick because of your actions, then you are missing the glory of the new covenant. If you believe that you're not healed because of an "open door" of sin, then your healing is dependent upon you and not Christ's finished work.

Galations 2:21 (KJV)
I do not frustrate the grace of GOD:
for if righteousness come by the law
then Christ is dead in vain

Galations 5:4 (KJV)
Christ is become of no effect unto you,
whosoever of you are justified by the law;
ye are fallen from grace.

It is by Christ's righteousness that we become co-heirs with Christ and thus sons of God. Therefore, without Christ's righteousness, healing is no longer ours. This is one reason why some people do not get healed. Actually, I will cover that in another chapter. Let's change gears for a minute. What if I showed you a statement that Jesus, Himself made? That should change our thinking!

It is commonly known, in the old covenant, that individual sin and disease have a relationship. However, Jesus made a statement that would contradict this long held belief. I am being real. This isn't a joke! Remember the man who was born blind from birth and the disciples asked Jesus whose sin it was that caused the man to be born blind? His answer was:

John 9:3 (KJV)
Jesus answered, Neither hath this man sinned
nor his parents: but that the works of God should
be made manifest in him.

Adding this together with Romans 5:13, it would appear that individual sin does not, in itself, lead to disease. The only other option would be that there were four sinless people on this earth at the time! This would mean the blind man and his parents would've fulfilled the law of Moses! We know that they were not without sin. The next sentence is the cause of confusion. We are all born that God's work would be manifested in us and through us. This is not saying that God gave this man blindness for this moment; God is light and in Him there is no darkness. He didn't give this man blindness, rather, this was a moment in which Jesus would reveal God's true nature, which is Love!

A more specific revelation is that the people Jesus was talking to believed that there were four miracles only the Messiah could perform. The orthodox Jews of that time period believed this, as does the present time orthodox Jew. The four miracles were leprosy, blind from birth, lame from birth, and the dead raised after seventy two hours. The Pharisees were well aware of this and that is why they hated Him. After each of these miracles were performed, Jesus placed emphasis on it for their benefit; saying "This is so the son of man might be glorified." Then the Pharisees took those people and harshly interrogated them. Remember what happened with Lazarus; they wanted to kill Lazarus, for this very reason.

Wrapping this chapter up, the points that need to be understood and remembered are that scripture undoubtedly shows the cause of death to be Adam's Sin, not individual sin. Therefore, death and all its source came from the first Adam, even murder and accidents! The second Adam, Christ Jesus, took care of Adam's sin and fulfilled the Law of Moses. Therefore, by His wounds you were healed, period! Why does disease and the causes of death still exist? The answer is upcoming in the following chapters. I know that this is a lot to process for some, but if you submit to this truth, you are healed!

2 THE ALL IN ONE CURE

Better get a full pot of coffee going, we now have the cause of disease (The sin of Adam), and any believer of Christ knows the solution........Jesus! If Jesus took care of it, then why isn't everyone healed? The answer is that our perception is off. We view healing as something that must be attained, and not as something that has already been achieved by the cross. Some recite the scripture "By His stripes we were healed", yet look at healing as if it must be acquired. We are not believing that we have already received it. This is a catch phrase, not an already accomplished truth. Jesus made it a possibility, but we must bring it into existence. This is where we err. This is where our perception is off. We say that it was finished at the Cross, but we look at it as if we have to bring healing into our reality. Here's the zinger......wait for it.......what applies to salvation applies to healing! What applies to healing applies to salvation. They are one in the same, there is no difference.

When we have an accurate understanding of this truth then many questions will be answered. Numerous false beliefs can be exposed in one massive swoop and we will no longer need to combat each false belief step-by-step. There is no need to focus on the lies when you believe the truth. People have spent years trying to understand why their healing hasn't come. They try to correct their beliefs bit, by painful bit and end up confused and feeling defeated. This is especially true for those who have seen many miracles.

Jesus used the physical things to receive the spiritual. The children of Israel were indeed more receptive to healing. They had experienced and seen miracles they could relate to, so Jesus used physical healing to show spiritual salvation. Now, let's take a look at salvation. Are you saved? How do you know that you are? Show me the physical evidence that you're saved. I'll give you a moment to think on this. First, if your answer is "I don't know", that is the wrong answer! Let's handle that right now!

ROMANS 10:9 (KJV)
That if thou shalt confess with thy mouth
the Lord Jesus, and shalt believe in thine
heart that God hath raised him from the dead
thou shalt be saved.

Good! Now with that handled, we can now say everyone answered yes to the first question. This is now settled and now, give me physical evidence. You cannot give me definite, physical proof can you? Yet, you can confidently state that you have salvation. How can that be? Here's how:

MATTHEW 21:22 (KJV)
And all things, whatsoever ye shall ask in prayer,
believing, ye shall receive.

Therefore, without any physical evidence, you can believe! What is your unit of measure for salvation? It is The Word of God. You now have HOPE, which is confident expectation, that you have salvation and eternal life. When does salvation start? Immediately, we aren't waiting for death. We have salvation as soon as we believe it in our heart. Healing is the same, there is no difference. Let's belabor this point for a moment. At the moment of salvation, when I believed in my heart that God raised Jesus from the dead, would it have been possible for my past sins to stop my salvation? NO! Can unforgiveness, stop salvation? NO! Is my salvation reliant upon God's timing? NO! Salvation, happens when I confess with my mouth and believe in my heart. What is the only thing that can stop salvation? Not believing in my heart or not confessing.......unbelief. That is it period, end of story! Healing and salvation are the same, therefore the same holds true for healing. If you believe in your heart you are saved, you are, and if you believe you're healed and healthy, you are.

PROVERBS 23:7(KJV)
For as he thinketh in his heart, so is he:

LUKE 6:45b (KJV)
for of the abundance of the heart
his mouth speaketh.

Without getting into the Greek too far, the Greek word for salvation means healed, saved, delivered, made whole and set free. It is all inclusive! Don't take my word for it, look it up for yourself! This isn't a scholarly book, cause I ain't no scholar! Let me show you another way to believe, that what applies to salvation also applies to healing.

Isaiah 53:1-5 (KJV)
"Who hath believed our report? And to whom
is the arm of the Lord revealed? For he shall
grow up before him as a tender plant, and as a
root out of a dry ground: he hath no form nor
comeliness; and when we shall see him, there is
no beauty that we should desire him.
He is despised and rejected of men; a man of sorrows,
and acquainted with grief: and we hid as it were our faces
from him; he was despised, and we esteemed him not.
Surely he hath borne our griefs, and carried our sorrows:
yet we did esteem him stricken, smitten of God,
and afflicted. But he was wounded for our transgressions,
he was bruised for our iniquities:
the chastisement of our peace was upon him;
and with his stripes we are healed."

Follow along with me: From "and when we shall see him" to "we are healed" this is not in chronological order. This is a description of what Jesus carried from the Garden of Gethsemane to His death. Part of the confusion lies in the translation with the use of the word "stripes" this word immediately makes us think of only the whipping post. Therefore, we think that our body was healed only at the whipping post. Therefore we treat healing as being separate from salvation and redemption. The Old English word for stripes means wounds, bruises; it is not a direct indication of whipping. To understand this correctly; it is by His wounds and bruises that we are healed. Jesus' first wound and blood was spilled when He was praying and He sweated blood. His body was broken, because the capillaries were busted. That was the start of Christ paying for everything. His body broken and His blood spilled from that moment on.

When Christ was taken into custody, the Roman soldiers beat him, more bruises and blood! Healing and salvation were paid for from start to finish.

Cement this into your heart, your healing wasn't just borne by Christ at the whipping post, but from the garden to Calvary, just as our redemption. I'll say it again, what applies to salvation, does in fact apply to healing!

Every step of the way, His body was broken and His blood was shed. There is no separation, as many teach. Salvation appears easier to believe because we view it as a future event. Therefore, I can claim that I am saved with no evidence. With healing, there is physical evidence. Therefore we come up with man's traditions as to why someone isn't healed which does not help people. Just like salvation, HEALING IS ALREADY DONE!

Nearly everyone believes that it is God's Will for every person to be saved. We teach that it is a personal decision and choice; even to the point of scoffing and insulting atheists, Muslims and others. Yet, when it comes to healing, we've developed the "God's Sovereignty theology". If someone doesn't get healed, then it is God's Sovereign will, not the sick person's choice. Let me try to put some honey on that statement. With salvation, if a person is living and conducting themselves in a lifestyle contrary to Christianity; which is an obvious sign of unbelief, we can opt out, and say "It's up to God to judge, if they truly are believers". There isn't that type of option with healing, and therefore out of sympathy we make theologies that aren't truth. TRUTH IS WHAT SETS A PERSON FREE! We need to speak it out, so more people will get healed. Sympathy will keep a person stuck where they are; compassion has the answer, Jesus! The moment a person confesses and believes in his heart that Jesus was raised from the dead, they are saved. The same is true for healing.

Salvation is available at any time for anyone. The same is true for healing. This can be and is proven scripturally, often. Jesus never once told anyone to come back at another time. To backup my argument against God's timing on healing, the following statement will be used. If God's timing is valid, then we don't believe "By His Stripes/Wounds we were Healed". Why then, aren't we healed? Because of unbelief! End of Story. Hold on for just a moment and don't get angry and close this book. Take a deep, deep breath and remember, this is Tony, I've been through it! If I can make the embarrassing statement "I was in unbelief, until I was healed", then you can have the humility to accept my statement. Here is some encouragement. you do have the faith to be healed! None of this is a lack of Faith!

My testimony proves that I could've been healed at anytime. Sitting in the wheelchair paralyzed and dying, having just been prayed for and the first thought that came to my mind was; "You are healed get up and walk". The second thought was "Idiot you're paralyzed, you can't walk". I believed the second thought, therefore I was in unbelief. I could've been healed at that moment had I grabbed a hold of the first thought. It was my choice and decision that kept me in that chair for two more agonizing years! This happened at least three times with varying thoughts. One time the thought was "If I'm healed then we'll lose my social security check and we'll lose everything!" Never thinking that if I was healed, then I could work!

One last point on the fact that healing is available for all people at any time. At the beginning of creation God spoke one time for the sun, moon and stars to be formed and their rotations set. One time He spoke it. Therefore, every day the sun and moon rise and set. He doesn't have to speak it into existence every day. It is the same with healing, He sent His Son for our salvation and healing one time. He spoke it one time, therefore it is available at all times!

Okay, let's put this tired puppy to bed. Here's what I want you to remember: your individual sin is not more powerful than Christ's sacrifice. It can't "block a healing". Secondly, what applies to salvation applies to healing, remember they are one and the same! Only one thing can stop both, Unbelief! You do have the faith, that isn't the issue!

This next chapter is going to be exciting! I will start to unravel the real reason why many believers don't get healed. I'm talking about believers that have a proven track record. They've seen perhaps even hundreds of people healed, yet they themselves are still sick. We point to them and say, "see they believe, yet they didn't get healed!" We can look at the great "anointed healers" and many of them died from disease. Why? If they died after seeing so many healed, then what hope is there for me? When we know the reason, we can arrive at the solution. We have an enemy that we fail to recognize in the proper context. In failing to recognize the correct enemy, we lose sight of the fact that it is already done. Literally, Christ defeated disease. It is not figuratively done, it's literally done, accomplished, defeated and over with! Yet, we don't recognize it, because of this one enemy. Let's get some coffee.

3 THE CONTROL CENTER

Let's talk about Adam and Eve, before the fall, they had a physical body. They interacted with the physical world, and were meant to live forever. They were also able to interact with God. They became enslaved to their physical senses, however with the lust of the eye on the fruit of the tree and subsequent disobedience. The serpent drew Eve's attention to the fruit and they literally took the bait. Before that time, their spirit controlled how they viewed the world, but after that moment, their physical senses took over.

GENESIS 3:6-7 (KJV)
And when the woman saw that the tree was
good for food, and that it was pleasant to
the eyes, and a tree to be desired to make one
wise, she took of the fruit thereof, and did eat
and gave also unto her husband with her; and
did eat. And the eyes of them both were opened,
and they knew that they were naked;

ROMANS 8:5 (KJV)
For they that are after the flesh do mind
the things of the flesh; but they that are
after the Spirit the things of the Spirit.

In the beginning, there was no such thing as time. Time, as we know, did not start until after Adam and Eve left the garden. This event did not happen immediately after God gave the command; an unknown period of time passed. How did the serpent tempt Eve? He did so by making her aware of it, and THEN she saw that it was good. This was with her eyes or physical senses. Their eyes were then opened and the carnal mind took over. What exactly is the carnal mind? Many people call it "flesh" or "sinful nature." Let's get more specific by gaining a real understanding of what happens with healing.

ROMANS 8:6 (KJV)
For to be carnally minded is death;
but to be spiritually minded is life and peace.

ROMANS 8:7 (KJV)
Because the carnal mind is enmity against God:
for it is not subject to the law of God, neither indeed can be.

We see then, that to be carnally minded is death. Using Adam and Eve as an example, when did their sin take place? It took place, when they made a choice based on their physical senses. Therefore, what is the carnal mind? What is the control center for the physical senses? The obvious answer, which would be correct, is the brain, because the brain is at enmity against God: "For it is not subject to the law of God, neither indeed can be." The brain is what the serpent used against both Adam and Eve. He threw a fiery dart of suggestion at them, a lie as it were. Eve's focus was then drawn to what her physical senses told her. The "sin nature" hadn't been borne yet, until Adam ate of the fruit. Before this moment in time, Adam and Eve while interacting with the physical world, were spiritually minded. They had life and peace. It was not until they made a decision based on their physical senses, which the brain is in charge of, that they became carnally minded and death entered the world. This isn't God punishing them, it was their own brain taking over.

Deep, deep breath my friends, this is crucial for you to understand, so I want your mind clear.

We are not our brains! Our thoughts do not originate in the physical body part we call the brain. Most people have an understanding that we are made up of two or three parts. Some say body, soul and spirit, others say body and soul. It's irrelevant to me. Since our spirit houses our soul, it makes no difference which way you choose to believe. Our body is what links us to the physical world. The brain is a part of the body and if you separate the brain from the body, they both die; however our spirit/soul continues to live. It is the soul (our spiritual mind), that is the true us.

The heart of the man is the link between the brain and the soul. (I'm snapping my fingers, snap, snap, snap), stay with me! The brain is a piece of equipment just like your arms or legs or kidneys. The brain only functions the way it was designed, to operate the physical body. The brain cannot understand the things of God and isn't subject to God, and neither can it be. This is why it is an enemy of God. It's a piece of equipment that satan uses against us, just as the serpent did to Adam and Eve. The enemy uses our physical senses to distract, tempt and destroy us. The end outcome will be determined on whether we make decisions based on our renewed mind/soul or from our physical senses. This is why the renewal of our mind is essential. The brain can't be renewed; it is our enemy.

Time for a cheerleading moment. Those who are In Christ, have the mind of Christ. Revelation of the above truth will lead to freedom; not only on a divinely healthy physical body, but spiritually as well. With this understanding comes true freedom and empowerment to live from the spirit and not from the carnal mind (brain). God's Grace: God's empowerment to do that which we cannot do. Our empowerment is Christ. Can I get an amen?! He whom the Son sets free, is free indeed! Christ has restored us. He is the second Adam in whom we have LIFE, and that life is Now!

1 JOHN 4:17 (KJV)
Herein is our love made perfect,
that we may have boldness in the day of judgment:
because as he is, so are we in this world.

Hopefully, (I confidently expect) you are convinced that the brain and our physical senses are at enmity with God. The next step is to prove that the brain does indeed lie or trick us. In fact, the devil uses our physical senses to lie to us through the device known as the brain. That is why we walk not by sight, but by faith (Trust). Paul meant this literally!

2 CORINTHIANS 5:7 (KJV)
For we walk by faith, not by sight:

Science has proven that our physical senses do not show us things as they really are. The brain mechanically fills in the blanks of what we perceive as reality, but it isn't. The secular world (scientists) will say that it is close enough to reality for us to rely on it. However, scriptures tell us that isn't the truth. Since this isn't a scientific book and yours truly isn't a scientist, sense (not common sense) will be used to prove this point. Our brain lies to us, to the point of death. Before I use the sensorial examples, I want to share a short fact; nearly all diseases are caused by the brain releasing too much of a certain chemical or the blood cells are causing something in the body to not be correct. We see the source as being outside the body, such as a germ. Yet, it's the brain's reaction to the "germ" that causes the disorder. True word!

Let's go through some examples of how our brains can lie to us. If you watch a person cut themselves, you will either feel the pain or experience some sort of physical reaction. This is your brain lying to you. If you were to put a fake arm in front of you and then someone hits the fake hand with a sledgehammer; you'll feel the pain in your real hand. Again, this is the brain lying to you. Put two blocks, one on top of the other, both being light grey in the exact same shade of color. The top one will appear to be light grey while the bottom block will be dark grey. The brain, again lying to you. These are simple experiments to conduct or you can research the internet and see scientific experiments that prove my point.

Now for some examples taken from people that I have prayed for. A man who had back problems so severe, that he could barely walk, after prayer, he started running around the gas station, thank You Jesus! A week later I ran into him, and he was worse off, so I asked him, "what happened?" He said that his doctor had shown him an MRI, taken months before, and this same doctor told him that if he even picked up a paperclip, he would be paralyzed. This led him to believe that he wasn't healed.

Another time, a woman who was suffering from a stroke, had her right arm paralyzed and stuck to her chest. I prayed for her and as she was talking to me, her arm was moving. As she observed her arm, it went right back to her chest. She sincerely had not seen it moving. I explained to her that she was healed and that it had moved. I prayed for her again, and this time she saw it. She acknowledged it and she was completely healed! Thank You Jesus.

Let me further explain the statement made prior to the above examples. It is man's carnal wisdom and knowledge that says the cause of sickness is an outside source. Medical knowledge is learned and taught from observation and experimentation. They take two or more bodies and assume, by observation, that one is healthy and the other is not. Then the same "professionals" make theories from these observations. They observe cells and then declare that one is healthy and the other is sick. Medicine is tested on subjects to determine whether they are effective or not. There is always a large degree of speculation. The whole of the medical establishment is built on man's knowledge. Can you explain why placebo's work? I can. It is called the finished work of Jesus.

1 CORINTHIANS 2:5 (KJV)
That your faith should not stand in the wisdom of men
but in the power of God.

2 CORINTHIANS 1:27 (KJV)
But God hath chosen the foolish things of the world
to confound the wise; and God hath chosen the weak
things of the world to confound the things which are mighty;

The wise men of this world walk by sight or better put, their physical senses. What happened in the garden was the physical brain and the physical senses were opened and took control. In Christ, all diseases are defeated. He bore them from the garden to the cross when He gave up His life. Jesus took them to hell and dropped them off and then was resurrected. We commonly do not believe that though, why? Well, because we look around and see people dying from disease. What is the difference between heaven and earth? In heaven, we won't have our brain deceiving us. With a renewed mind and with this knowledge, we can experience this now on earth. It is done, now we only have to believe it.

Let's have some coffee and afterward let's hit a very hot topic. The diet theology! DISCLAIMER: In the following, I am not recommending a certain diet, nor am I telling you to abandon a "healthy" diet. Let's not be stupid. I am not responsible for unintelligent decisions that you may choose to make, nor am I telling you not to listen to your doctor. I respect the medical field; they do prolong lives.

The purpose of this section of the book, is to point out the difference, and frailty, of the wisdom of man, and give you a different perspective. I survived six to four months with a paralyzed stomach, the medical term is gastroparesis. I had no nutrition whatsoever; no intravenous feeding, no feeding tube, no sustenance and yet, The Lord Jesus sustained me until my healing. We need to change our perspective that certain foods will keep us healthy. It really isn't what we put into our mouths that keeps us healthy, it is what we believe that will keep us healthy.

Matthew 15:11 (NLT)
It's not what goes into your mouth that defiles you,
you are defiled by the words that come out of your mouth

Many preachers and religious leaders claim a healthy diet is God's plan.

According to them, eating correctly is your responsibility. This viewpoint gives credit to you for your health. This particular way of thinking fails miserably. You may ask, why? Let me tell you why, because there are thousands of people in hospitals that eat correctly according to human wisdom. A certain diet never did and never will keep anyone healthy. Again, I am not advocating an unhealthy diet, but what I am stating is that we need to change our focus from relying on food to relying on Christ's finished work. We need to trust that, His body that was broken for our body, keeps us healthy. In the new covenant, there are no dietary restrictions. We spend millions of dollars, time and energy making sure we eat correctly. When all we have to do is to sanctify the food, by the authority of Christ, which will sustain us.

What doctors tell us is a healthy diet, changes every day. One minute eggs are unhealthy and the next day they are now healthy. The limit on coffee was two cups a day, but now doctors say that six cups is actually good for you. All of this is based on the physical senses, yet we are convinced that if we eat correctly we stay healthy, this is just not true. Diet has become a huge distraction, keeping us from focusing on our Heavenly Father and Jesus.

When we rely on the proper diet to maintain our health, we aren't believing that Christ gave His body, for ours.

MATTHEW 6:25 (KJV)
Therefore I say unto you, take no thought
for your life, what ye shall eat,
or what ye shall drink; nor yet
for your body, what ye shall put
on. Is not the life more than meat,
and the body than raiment?

Yet, we as believers spend hours researching diet. We spend thousands of dollars planning our diets, and that isn't what Jesus taught.

MARK 7:18-20 (KJV)
And he saith unto them, Are ye so without
understanding also? Do ye not perceive,
that whatsoever thing from without entereth
into the man, it cannot defile him;
Because it entereth not into his heart,
but into the belly, and goeth out into the
draught, purging all meats?

And he said, That which cometh out
of the man, that defileth the man.

What comes from the heart and out of the mouth is what causes us to become sick.

PROVERBS 18:21 (KJV)
Death and life are in the power of the tongue:
and they that love it shall eat the fruit thereof.

PROVERBS 18:21 (TV)
Death is in the power of the tongue:
and they that love death shall it the fruit of it.
Life is in the power of the tongue:
and they that love life shall it the fruit of it.

It isn't what you put into your mouth that kills you and causes diseases, it is what you speak. Get this into your heart! There is ample scriptural support for this, yet most choose to rely on physical things to stay healthy. Here is the kicker; in the new testament Paul agrees. In fact, he calls commanding abstinence from certain foods "doctrines of demons." When a doctor tells you to abstain from a certain food, this falls under his very warning. Take strong note of this:

1 TIMOTHY 4:1-5 (NLT)
Now the Holy Spirit tells us clearly
that in the last times some will turn away
from the true faith; they will follow deceptive spirits
and teachings that come from demons.
These people are hypocrites and liars, and
their consciences are dead.
They will say it is wrong to be married and
wrong to eat certain foods.
But God created those foods to be eaten
with thanks by faithful people who know the truth.
Since everything God created is good,
we should not reject any of it
but receive it with thanks. For we know it is made
acceptable, by the word of God and prayer.

DISCLAIMER: I am not advocating a poor diet. Don't think for a moment you can read this and then eat in gluttony without consequences.

My purpose in this isn't to get you to change your diet, it is to change your focus. Do you have hope (confident expectation) in what you put into your body? Or is it in Christ's Sacrifice, He gave His Body for you to be completely healthy, healed, whole, set free and saved!

There are those who advocate that "diet" is the way to stay healthy, stating that God shows us a "healthy" diet through essentially three ways; Daniel's fast, one additional scripture and will also say that through the Law of Moses God showed us what our diet should look like. Jesus and Paul both showed us otherwise, as I have already revealed.

Daniel's fast shows us the complete opposite of what is traditionally claimed. Daniel's fast tells us to rely on God to keep us healthy, not on the wisdom of men. In spite of the wisdom of their day that stated a diet of mainly meat would make them healthy; Daniel went against it and the Lord sustained him, in spite of their so-called "wisdom". Yes, Daniel did do this to avoid eating meat sacrificed to idol's, because He was under the Law of Moses. However, it wasn't God pointing us to keep ourselves healthy, rather to rely on Him.

The scripture used to support the "diet theology":

ONE CORINTHIANS 6:18-20 (KJV)
Flee fornication. Every sin that a man doeth
is without the body; but he that committeth
fornication sinneth against his own body.
What? Know ye not that your body is the temple
of the Holy Ghost which is in you, which ye have
of God, and ye are not your own?

To prove a point, people misuse this verse out of pride. In this verse, Paul is clearly talking about the sin of fornication which is the only sin that is committed within our body. This verse does not even hint that you are responsible, through diet, to maintain the temple of the Holy Spirit. As a result of this, continue to eat as you are presently but rely on Christ's Sacrifice to maintain a divinely healthy body. It is done, we need only believe it! In fact, I do recommend taking communion as you eat the food. Remember, the only way we maintain perfect health or have now come into perfect health, is by Him giving us His broken body for ours!

To sum this all up: Adam and Eve, before the fall, were able to walk by the Spirit while interacting with the physical world. Now, IN Christ through His Holy Spirit we can too. The revelation that the brain and our physical senses are at enmity with God will help; but only with a change of what our heart believes and a renewing of the mind. This knowledge will not only help us to receive our healing, but we can also live a sanctified lifestyle through this fact, that in Christ we are empowered!

The main points to remember:
1. Healing is included in salvation: salvation is already done, once we accurately believe it.
2. THE BRAIN: Our physical senses are what tells us that it isn't done.
3. We already have the victory In Christ.
4. We walk by faith not by literal sight.

The next chapter is going to start revealing some answers. It will also show errors in how we approach healing. This may seem overwhelming but take encouragement in the fact that healing is always available. Take a short break and submit these things to your heart. You do this by thinking about them and accepting them as TRUTH. Got to run to the store and get some coffee!

4 METHODS OF MADNESS

OH boy! This is going to be a doozy, better have a full pot of coffee right beside you. This is going to bust so many bubbles and possibly hurt a lot of feelings. Sorry in advance. The healing ministry is made up of many factions and different beliefs; which makes for a lot of confusion and frustration. In order to get to the milk out of a coconut, you gotta use a screwdriver and a sledgehammer, busting right through the tough outer shell. We've already discussed how salvation and healing are one in the same. If you are hard-headed and still don't see it then, you may want to stop reading. Put the book down, now, throw it in the trash and walk away, quickly; because this won't help you. There is one method by which you attain salvation.

ROMANS 10:9 (KJV)
That if thou shalt confess with thy mouth
the Lord Jesus, and shalt believe in thine
heart that God hath raised him from the dead
thou shalt be saved.

There is only one method for salvation and only one method for healing. In regard to salvation there is only one way we believe in our heart. This way is that through His resurrection, Christ earned your salvation. The same goes for healing. Accept Christ's sacrifice and then you are saved AND have eternal life. From the garden to His resurrection, Jesus earned our complete salvation. People take different paths to get there and for many it takes years. For myself, it took forty three years and lots of struggles and sad to say, many do not ever get to that point. There is no difference in healing or salvation, it's one in the same. Yet with salvation, we blame the person (for not believing in Christ) and with healing we blame God. I am just pointing out how completely the same the two are; yet how completely different we treat the different circumstances. There is one method to salvation and the method is the same for healing. It is called the finished work of Jesus, the atonement or the cross. People often will state that Jesus heals by different methods. This is wrong on two accounts:

1. They singularly look to "by his wounds you were healed" figuratively speaking and so they're already in unbelief.
2. They have no idea what a method is.

Our heavenly Father has only one method of healing, and it was done from the garden to the resurrection. The definition of a method being used is: A procedure or process to obtain a specific end result, or object. In this case, the specific objective is healing and that procedure was finished two thousand years ago at Cavalry. It is OUR perception that is off my friends. I'm hearing ya say, "Well, Mr. Tony, Sir, I beg to differ, Jesus used many different ways to get a person healed". First and foremost, don't call me sir or Mr. "I work for a living!" Just plain ol Tony will do. Secondly, no He didn't! Jesus performed different actions, not different methods. Also we must take into account, that this was before the cross and was the children's bread; meaning the children of Israel. After the Cross, it is for everyone who believes. At the Last Supper, Jesus points straight to His broken body and not to the children's bread; but to Himself, the bread of life! He took the bread and broke it gave thanks and said "This is my body which is broken for you. Do this in remembrance of me". In other words, remember my broken body that I gave as a propitiation for your body, remember my blood that seals you into the new covenant.

Why all the different actions? That is quite simple, He used them to take the person's attention off of their physical senses, off of the symptoms. It was a distraction. The majority of the time with the specific accounts, were people that didn't come to him, such as the man born blind from birth. He put mud made from spit on his eyes and made the blind man walk across town. I am sure that fella was muttering underneath his breath. The lunatic boy's father, due to the disciples failure, had brought his son but was in unbelief. The ten lepers did come to Him, but He sent them to the temple to be checked out by the priest and I'm sure that got them talking on the way. In each account, a distraction was needed. Even Peter used this action with the lame man at the gate called Beautiful. The last thing that man expected was to be yanked up off the ground. Smith Wigglesworth used this action as well. It takes their focus off of the symptoms and puts the brain into shock for a second; long enough for the person to acknowledge that the symptoms are gone. Many people call it an act of faith, it isn't. It is an action that takes the person's focus off of their physical senses. We'll go into more details on this in a future chapter.

The only method needed to attain healing has already been performed, accomplished, done and finished at the cross. Healing itself has already been attained. When we really understand this, then divine health and a sanctified lifestyle follow. People do get healed from other methods, yes! They really do, but the problem is without the revelation that it is already attained for us, we continually face one health crisis after another and it turns into a vicious cycle. Also, we can fall prey to traps, lies and snares within the other methods. Let me state a couple of things here: healing and deliverance aren't separate ministries, they are one in the same. Every evil thing has the same source the father of lies. A demon is a spirit that carries a lie, so everything I'm saying applies to the same. Every cause of sickness is demonic because it is a lie. What it all boils down to is the lie that we aren't healed and that sickness still has power. How is a lie defeated; by TRUTH. SALVATION in it's true definition is healed, saved, set free, made whole, which have been attained at the cross and is available to all now. When we have the revelation of this, we are no longer striving to get something. Therefore, when I pray for someone, I am merely speaking truth and therefore the lie is dispelled. I feel no burden, because Jesus accomplished it, I didn't. Nor do I place any burden on the person that I'm praying for because it's already done. They just have to acknowledge it. The problem is the physical senses and the way people use them as a gauge of whether they are healed or not. When we use the gauge of our physical senses (ie. the symptoms, we still see, feel, taste, touch, hear the symptoms) then people decide they are not healed.

PROVERBS 23:7(KJV)
For as he thinketh in his heart, so is he:

MATTHEW 21:21 (KJV)
Verily I say unto you, if ye have faith, and doubt not

The scripture above in Proverbs works both ways, so if you think in your heart, that you're still sick, then you are. That is what happens when the gauge for healing is the brain or physical senses. When we place the gauge on our physical senses, we just doubted. This leads to all kinds of methods to "achieve" healing. We start looking for reasons why it didn't work, and we have just walked away from the TRUTH, that it is done. We then search for actions or things that "blocked" our healing. We can't block something that's already been done. We can't un-bake a pizza. Yet, that is what all other methods do, they promote a lie.

Okay, before we get too deep into this, let me be clear, if you were healed by one of the methods that I am going to completely tear down, the healing is still legitimate. It still happened because of Jesus' finished work. The problem is that there is still a lie that is being believed. Don't get all defensive on me. If you presently minister to others by one of these methods, prove to yourself through the Holy Spirit, that I'm right and then stop ministering that way. No need to get all defensive either, just recognize and discern truth.

Anything can become a method. If I consider that in order for a person to get healed, I have to say a specific word every time.. then that is a method. A very popular method is "Inner Healing" there are many different types and forms of this. When I'm referring to Inner Healing, I am speaking of the kind where you must ensure all doors to sin are closed. Soul ties are broken, soul wounds repented of and in many cases generational curses are broken. This often times will also include Masonic curses, ties to witchcraft etc. This method also includes, in many cases, visualization...error, wrong, get outta that wicked thing. By the way, I was certified in Inner Healing one form of this, so I am well aware and have intimate knowledge of this practice. I'm not speaking from an uninformed viewpoint here.

If you believe a lie you get the lie. If you believe in generational curses then it does exist for you. Indeed, even in the secular world they teach this lie......it's called heredity/genetics which comes from where? You guessed it, the carnal mind or the brain. Four generations have suffered from diabetes, therefore based on physical observation there is a gene that causes this, another lie perpetuated, from the physical senses. It's medically proven, Tony, they've isolated the gene (being sarcastic), of course they have. That is man's wisdom and it's foolishness. We walk by faith, not by sight. Our gene pool is from Jesus.

ROMANS 8:5 (KJV)
For they that are after the flesh do mind
the things of the flesh;

Should it come as a shock, that physical things prove physical things?

PROVERBS 14:12 (KJV)

There is a way which seemeth right unto a man,
but the end thereof are the ways of death.

Of course the physical senses prove the physical things. The road to them are death, when Christ is the bread of life!

Let's spend a moment on "generational curses" and all the things that apply to it such as the Masonic curse etc... The scripture that is used to support this is:

DEUTERONOMY 5:9-10b (KJV)
for I the Lord thy God am a jealous God,
visiting the iniquity of the fathers upon
the children unto the third and fourth
generation. Of them that hate me,
and shewing mercy unto thousands of
them that love me and keep my
commandments.

This scripture firstly is under The Law of Moses and applied only to the children of Israel. The curse applied to those who bowed down to idols. Also to those who hate God. Yet, if one argues against that, here is where God rescinds that.

EZEKIEL 18:20 (KJV)
The soul that sinneth, it shall die.
The son shall not bear the iniquity
of the father, neither shall the father
bear the iniquity of the son:
the righteousness of the righteous
shall be upon him, and the wickedness
of the wicked shall be upon him.

GALATIANS 3:13 (KJV)
Christ hath redeemed us from the curse
of the law, being made a curse for us:
for it is written, cursed is every one that
hangeth on a tree:

You see, there are no generational curses; unless you believe that there are. Proof of that is below. In the following scripture Paul states exactly that: if you believe in the Law and live by the Law; then you live in the consequences of The LAW.

GALATIONS 3:12 (KJV)
And the law is not of faith: but, the man that
doeth them shall live in them.

Take a moment to ponder these things. A pot of coffee will help, also take a deep breath. The biggest lie of the "Inner Healing" method is coming up next.

THE LIE: It is by your sin that you became sick. It is by your actions that you will be healed. Inner Healing implies directly and indirectly that you are the cause of your sickness, therefore you are the solution. You must dig up your past and find some sin. This sin opened the door to the devil, and you must shut it. In other words: Your actions blocked what Christ did for you! This is a lie from the pit of hell and makes the cross of no effect for you!

Galations 5:4 (KJV)
Christ is become of no effect unto you,
whosoever of you are justified by the law;
ye are fallen from grace.

Justified by your actions! We then wonder why we aren't healed, instead of by His wounds you were healed. It just became by your repentance you were healed. Instead of a free gift, it was just made into a work and you earned your healing. Do you see what utter nonsense this is? Now, let me now glory in the Lord! The Lord is so merciful and His healing so available. In spite of all of this, people have been healed through this method! Yet, not because of the method. It was because of the cross and the person believed they were healed.

This is how horrendous the method of Inner Healing is: A woman was diagnosed with stage four cancer. She went to a Inner Healing session. She was married, but prior to their marriage, she and her husband had lived together. She was told that she had cancer because they had sex before they were married. She repented of it, less than four months later she died.

Granted most Inner Healing ministers have more tact than that. This example is used to show how repugnant the "Inner Healing" method is. Yet that is exactly, what this method implies. You caused your sickness therefore it is by your actions you will be healed. This is utter nonsense and the proof is right in front of us. If by repenting the woman would be healed then the devil had no cause to give her the cancer in the first place. She had repented, before the cancer occurred. Proof of this is the fact that this man and woman had gotten married before she became ill. They had repented. Repentance is simply recognizing your error, changing your mind and your actions. That happened.

Soul Ties: This is boulder-dash, nonsense, pure hog-wash and utter stupidity. You must separately repent for every person you've ever slept with. They teach that, even if it was before you were a believer, you must sever the bond between yourselves. Often using words to the effect "with the sword of The Spirit I sever the soul ties". What if I don't remember every person I slept with? "Oh the Holy Spirit knows". Then why do I have to go through this with the ones I do remember? Here's the thing, repenting is changing your mind, thereby changing your actions.

Repentance, most inner healing ministries have you ask Holy Spirit what you need to repent of. If you are no longer doing that particular sin, if you had decided it was wrong and stopped doing it. You have repented from it.

HEBREWS 8:12 (KJV)
For I will be merciful to their unrighteousness,
and their sins and their iniquities will I remember
no more.

Therefore, if you have repented from it, God is merciful and will remember your sin no more. If this is true, then how can Holy Spirit bring forward a sin you are no more actively doing? Also, bringing back to your memory the first thing we discussed, death entered the world through sin; the sin of the first Adam. The Second Adam has taken that away from those who Believe. If individual sin does in fact block a healing, and the Holy Spirit is indeed recalling a past sin, then why aren't more people healed through "Inner Healing" and why does it take so long for a person to "work through" their sins, to attain full closure? It is because it is man's method, not The Father's. The Father's method was Christ! It is done, now just believe it! There is nothing more powerful than the atonement, sin cannot stop healing. The only thing that stops a healing is not believing that you are healed! Many people spend years and years going through all their past sins. and yet, never receive their healing. It is time we stop with man's methods and use Christ's. Believe a lie, you get the lie. If you believe that an individual sin is more powerful then Christ's Body broken for you, then it is because you are searching for that one sin you've forgotten about. Or you get mad at your spouse, you think it's a sin and therefore no healing for you. Healing then is dependent upon your action, Not on Christ.

Let me wrap up on "Inner Healing" with this statement. If sin could block a healing, I would've never been healed. God is no respecter of persons. Therefore, the fact that I was healed, with active sin, totally destroys, that whole inner healing thing. I was actively sinning on many points. Unforgiveness, yup there were many people that were on my "hit list" that I hated. My thoughts were very impure. I was actively lying to my wife about a number of things, all of which I came clean on about four months later. Which proves another point, I kept my healing in spite of all of that! The difference, my head hadn't been filled with the lies of men. No one had told me that I couldn't be healed, because of my sin. Once again, the DISCLAIMER: WE SHOULD BE LIVING SANCTIFIED LIVES. IN FACT, PAUL STATES THAT THOSE LIVING IN THE SPIRIT WILL NOT COMMIT THE LUSTS OF THE FLESH! In no way am I advocating that it is ok to sin! When we realize what we have in the new covenant we won't sin. When we understand that we are empowered to not sin, we won't. Do not misunderstand me, repentance is of absolute necessity. Acknowledge your wrongs and stop doing them! That is true repentance!

Now, the next method that many of you do not know about. It is gaining popularity, but is totally unscriptural. Please use your God given, earned by Jesus, discernment and avoid this next method at all costs! It is called the Courtrooms of Heaven. This is a teaching that states in order to be healed, you must visit the courtrooms of heaven and have a judgment rendered in your favor. This method uses vain imagination or visualization. It is very presumptive and makes broad assumptions. The main scripture out of a total of three it uses is Job. Where the sons of God gather and God asks satan what he is up to. Satan then accuses Job and because Job is not present, God finds him guilty. Therefore satan is allowed to terrorize Job. Job was not under any covenant with God. Since then, we have Jesus! This totally denies Christ's finished work. Once again, this puts your healing on your action not based on the cross. This method pulls people in by the use of the imagination and, use of the five physical senses. If it isn't simple it isn't Christ.

2 CORINTHIANS 11:3 (KJV)
But I fear, lest by any means, as the serpent
beguiled Eve through his subtilty, so your minds
should be corrupted from the simplicity that is in Christ.

Enough said about that method.

There are other methods men use to try to attain healing; Reiki, healing hands, New Age methods. People do get healed by them. Without Christ, these methods are not sustainable and the reason is that without Christ, people fall prey to unbelief. A far worse thing often happens to them, the same as the above methods. Inner Healing and the courtrooms are extremely complicated and in the case of the courtrooms, those using this method are actually warned about doing it inappropriately. I call these "a method", because they are trying to get someone healed. They feel that healing has been blocked, and therefore not attained for the person. Wrong! Healing was attained for us at the cross, a free gift which can't be blocked, but can be refused and not received because of "teachings." This next "method" may or may not be considered a "method" depending on the person. We are now going to discuss "Anointed Healers" or healing evangelists. Categorically, nothing is wrong with having another person pray for you. Healing services, themselves are very good. Many people get healed this way! Indeed, yours truly has had healing services. The caution is how they are presented; boasting or equipping? If people are attracted to the minister because they have a "special anointing", then they are boasting of themselves. The anointing is the Holy Spirit, Whom we all have. We can all pray for the sick and see them healed. Many will claim a one hundred percent success rate, to attract people. Many will also give testimony after testimony of people they've prayed for who got healed. Most, do not have a clue and think that they are giving a person something the person doesn't have access to. They believe they have achieved that person's healing for them. Indeed, even the people going believe this. They hear how a certain person has a good success rate and flock to them to be healed.

Here's the danger, we then look to a person, for healing and not at the cross where we have it, already. The other danger is that we perceive it like this and then our healing isn't secure based on our belief. Coupled with the fact that many "anointed healers" look at it the same way, that they attained your healing for you. Please do not mistake this to say that I am against either the healing services or the minister. Another thing is the thought that because "so and so" walks in power then it is looked upon as if God is confirming the person. Then even in spite of lifestyle or theology, this person becomes a mouthpiece for God. Extreme danger! Although a person walks in healing it is not an automatic sign that they are living a sanctified lifestyle or have correct theology. It is a confirmation of Christ and His accomplishment on the cross. Healing is always available and all believers can pray for the sick and see people healed. It is not based on a person's actions. Any person who believes can heal the sick. Any person who has the baptism of The Holy Spirit is anointed for all the gifts.

ACTS 10:38 (KJV)
How God anointed Jesus of Nazareth
with the Holy Ghost and with power:
who went about doing good, and healing
all that were oppressed of the devil;
for God was with him.

ACTS 1:8 (KJV)
But ye shall receive power, after that the
Holy Ghost is come upon you: and ye shall
be witnesses unto me both in Jerusalem,
and in all Judaea, and in Samaria,
and unto the uttermost part of the earth.

ACTS 2:16-17 (KJV)
But this is that which was spoken
by the prophet Joel;
And it shall come to pass in the last days,
saith God, I will pour out of my Spirit upon all flesh:

There is one anointing and that is The Holy Spirit. It started with Jesus, and then on the day of Pentecost His Spirit was poured out upon all flesh. No one has more or less of Holy Spirit, we have the fullness of Him within us. Take note in Acts, Peter states that the prophecy made by Joel was fulfilled, it has happened. There is one gift, that is The Holy Spirit with many manifestations of Him. This is spoken about in Corinthians. Paul does name nine gifts and these gifts are available to all who have been baptized in The Holy Spirit. I just want to make mention of that, because some of you will question that right away. My point is that we are all anointed with His Holy Spirit. Do not get "Callings" confused with what people refer to as "The anointing". We are each called to do life differently, yet every believer can and should walk in healing.

MARK 16:17 (KJV)
And these signs shall follow them that believe;
In my name shall they cast out devils; they shall
speak with new tongues; they shall take up serpents;
and if they drink any deadly thing, it shall not hurt them;
they shall lay hands on the sick, and they shall recover.

5 THE FORMULA OF HEALING

Many people will often try to tell me that there are no formulas to healing. The people that make this statement are warning people to not come up with a formula based off of experience only. Our experiences, up to this point, are not going to match up to Jesus', so coming up with a formula based on our experience is very dangerous. Indeed, this is how all these wrong methods come about, through experience and leaning on our physical senses. Yet, there is a formula that is set up by Christ and Paul. The method by which healing was attained for us is the cross. There is one formula which is scriptural: love, believe, expect and receive. This is a Christ-given formula, told to us time and time again. It is applicable in all areas of salvation or in other words, in all aspects of a believer's life.

It is at this point where we start tying everything we've discussed so far, together, and we will conclude with the pretty little ribbon that was promised. Sticking with this formula will keep you from being led astray by the other methods that were mentioned in the previous chapter. Stick with this and apply it, not only for yourself, but when praying for others as well. I am going to spend a lot of time clarifying this, so it will be firmly established in your mind.

First, I want to share how this formula was brought to realization in my life. This will also answer any questions of how this is biblical. Then, in the following three chapters, we will investigate the terms believe, expect, receive, and love individually. Strap yourself into your seat, open you heart to this and have a full pot of coffee on hand.

My healing, especially as studying scripture for the first time, left me puzzled. At the time of my healing, in my opinion, I had no faith for healing, much less being able to command my own healing. How in the world was I healed? There were many people that heard my testimony and made presumptions. I heard everything from "you gave up and gave it to God" which was nonsense. I had literally given up, yes; but I hadn't given it to God. I tried to kill myself, and that is not giving it to God! Another theory was, that God had a sovereign plan for me; which is true, our loving Father does have a plan for each of us. We have a choice though and decide whether we want to go along with His plan. Nothing just sovereignly happens, against our will. The context of this presumption is that no matter what I did or choices that I made my healing would have happened regardless. This is so wrong! If that were the case, that healing just sovereignly happens (or even salvation), then no one would die from disease.

While studying scriptures and asking Holy Spirit to show me how in the world my healing happened, bit by bit He revealed it to me. Reminder: I was learning this on my own for the first year and a half and had never heard of the current preachers that teach healing. It was just myself, the scriptures and Holy Spirit. During this time, I was praying for the sick everyday with amazing results. Yet, I still wanted answers, so that my ministering to others, would become more effective.

The desire of my heart, is for everyone to know how readily available healing is. Roughly two weeks after my healing, I was supposed to give my testimony to a group of people. The night before, I started experiencing intense pain in my stomach. The pain was so bad that it had me curled up in a ball on the floor. Since I had been awake all night and in immense pain, I texted the pastor and told him I couldn't make it. That was around six in the morning and we were scheduled to meet at nine. I had wanted so badly to share my testimony. Anger hit me and a thought arose; I had just been healed from a paralyzing disease how could I let a tummy ache (minimizing the pain), stop me? Curled up in a ball on the floor, I forced myself up on my knees and started to praise the Father and Jesus. Within minutes, all pain left my body and pure joy hit me. I went to that meeting and it was amazing!

Three things happened while I was laying on the floor. These weren't conscience thoughts, they were a reaction to a lie. First, I refused to believe that the situation was hopeless. There would be no entertaining thoughts of "I will just have to live with the pain." I minimized the pain by calling it a little tummy ache, instead of recognizing how severe it was. There was an expectation that the pain had to leave. Mistakenly, I assumed it was my praising and worshiping, that God had rewarded.

A few weeks after that incident, I woke up absolutely depleted of strength. I was dizzy, nauseous and could not stand up. Thinking back to the stomach pain, I started to praise and worship the Father and Jesus again. Nothing happened, but I was bound and determined to not let this keep me down. Crawling out to the car, I headed to work. Let me comment here that driving was the last thing I should have done. About an hour later, I informed my boss that I needed to go home. Frustrated and angry and in intense agony, I crawled into bed. My mind was swimming with questions; "What in the world, why hadn't the pain, weakness, dizziness left?" I had done the same thing as before. Passing out in the bed, I fell asleep. When I woke up, my condition was the same. My thoughts then went back to when I was paralyzed, and how I had declared that the Lord would heal me. Nothing had happened then, and for two years I had continued my spiral downhill to death.

Convinced that it is always God's will for us to be healed, I grabbed my bible. I asked Holy Spirit to show me what I was doing wrong. In my weakened, sick state, I don't even remember what I read. Suddenly it dawned on me, that back then, I had thought that I would be healed based on my declaration. I had done the very same thing with this attack. I was basing my being healed, on my action. I had thought that because I was praising and worshipping, God would reward my action. Then I came across the scripture:

MATTHEW 21:22 (KJV)
And all things, whatsoever ye shall ask
in prayer, believing, ye shall receive.

MARK 11:24 (KJV)
Therefore I say unto you, what things
soever ye desire, when ye pray, believe that
ye receive them, and ye shall have them.

Thinking on these scriptures, I remembered how I had been healed, and it had been when I had commanded my body. This time I simply said, "sickness go, energy and health return", and then I passed out. When I woke up, I felt so much better. I started to understand what these scriptures meant. When you declare something, already knowing it was done, then it happens. It is not based on the actions that a person takes but rather, what you believe per situation, seemed to be vital.

I took this new awareness with me during my street ministering. Every time I ministered to anyone, I consciously believed they had their healing already. I would see them in my mind as a healed person. Then I would say, "you're healed, now move it." I was now speaking, knowing that the person was already healed or not even actually sick at all. Amazing things were happening.

Next I decided, once again, to learn from experience. I hated having to wear glasses, just really hated anything on my face and so I became determined to have my vision restored. This was about a month after my healing and so I did what had become familiar to me and commanded my eyes to be fully restored. Taking off my bi-focals, (ugh- still blurry), I still couldn't read, or see things at a distance. I set the glasses down on the night-stand and went outside to do some yard work. Ariel, our hound/golden retriever, decided to make them her lunch and when I went back inside they were no longer useable. A three hundred dollar set of glasses destroyed! Well, for me, that was that! I was not going to pay another three hundred dollars for a new set. My wife was laughing with me when I told her what happened. I also told her, " There will be no buying another set, my eyes are already healed", yet still blurry! Day after day, they were still blurry but meanwhile my nose was buried in the scriptures, trying to make sense of it. I was also still seeing amazing miracles, legs growing out, broken bones healed, HIV healed, hepatitis C healed. All these amazing things happening, yet my eyes were still messed up. What was I doing wrong? I would repeat, "by his stripes I was healed" and make all sorts of wonderful declarations, yet no improvement.

At this same time, there was a growth on my arm that had been there for years. I was working on that as well with no change or improvement. Meanwhile, I was still thinking that it had to be a lack of faith. My faith had to increase. I did just as the man with the lunatic son, "Lord, I believe help my unbelief" "Lord, please give me more faith". I did all that stuff and this went on for about a month. Maybe I was wrong, and there were certain things God just wouldn't heal. Thinking this way, I started falling into many of the same dire conclusions that others had, until one day, this scripture came to me. The Lord highlighted it to me and there was no ignoring it.

HEBREWS 11:1 (KJV)
Now faith is the substance of things hoped for,
the evidence of things not seen.

I did a word search on faith and hope and out of that word search, and Holy Spirit's nudging, came the starting of a realization. That belief plus hope equals proof of faith. I was remembering back to that wonderful day my original healing happened and for the first time, I was seeing the full picture. It was as if the Holy Spirit had finally answered my question, about how and why I was healed that day!

My vision had started out with Jesus being scourged, but then it shifted to the cross. The scourging had shown me, without my being conscience of it, His love for us and that He paid for the fullness of our salvation. The cross had shown me the very thing that was killing me being put to death. Jesus became sin therefore all the plagues of death entered into Him. I saw the brass serpent and that when Moses erected it, the children of Israel gazed upon it. They saw what was killing them, being killed and therefore, they were healed. In my vision, that's what happening even though I didn't know it then. This created hope in me as I saw His Love, believed He had paid for and accomplished my healing, and then had HOPE. Hope is defined as confident expectation, the end result being faith and together being made substance. It was then, that this realization became a revelation. All of a sudden I could read without the magnifying glass that I had been using. I looked at a distant clock and could see it. I looked down at the growth on my arm, and it had dramatically decreased in size and the next day it was completely gone!

The right belief with expectation equaled the manifestation, of what is expected from the heart. This results in faith becoming substance. I took this out into the streets while ministering to people. Now, I had always given my testimony, but now I was doing it to create expectation (Hope) in others. I was starting to see a few things: I could get results without creating this hope, but then the next day the symptoms would return in that person. Creating hope within a person first, seemed to be more effective. After all, that is what happened with me; the right belief and then expecting something to happen, and then the pain left. This had all been created within my heart, without my conscience thought, by the vision of Christ's finished work.

That is just the beginning of understanding what happens below the surface when anyone gets healed. As time went along and my experiences grew, I started seeing others things. I started listening to other teachings and some confirmed the truth I had learned. In the next three chapters we are going to unlock believe, hope and faith and how each of these things directly impact someone being healed or not.

6 UNQUESTIONABLE FACT

It's time to check yourself, have your symptoms decreased? If they have acknowledge it, "Thank You Jesus"! Go by your very first reaction, or you will rationalize yourself right out of your healing. Do you have your coffee ready? Let's get started then. Simple is best, simple is plain and easy to understand and simple definitions are even better. My definition of the word believe is simply "taking something as an unquestionable fact". We tend to lump believing and faith into one definition, but they are not the same thing. Faith, in its simplest term, is trust. Believing, is taking something as an unquestionable fact. Where healing is concerned, there are two similar levels of beliefs (unquestionable fact), that need to be cemented into your very being. The first we already discussed; that Jesus bore our diseases and was resurrected from the dead. The second one is more specific, we must take this as an unquestionable fact; that the disease we are facing is gone and we are healed. We need to do this even before we see the symptoms leave.

ROMANS 10:9-10 (KJV)
That if thou shalt confess with
thy mouth the Lord Jesus, and shalt
believe in thine heart that God hath raised
him from the dead, thou shalt be saved. For
with the heart man believeth unto righteousness;
and with the mouth confession is made unto salvation.
[Salvation includes healing]

The words saved or salvation (sozo) has healing included in their definition. It is in Christ's righteousness that we have all things and with the mouth confession is made to wholeness.

We take many things as fact and many of those are based upon our physical senses. When we truly take something as a fact, it is nearly impossible to be talked out of that belief. There are examples of this all around us. When a person is totally convinced of something, you can approach that person with solid facts, lay it all out on the line, show them statistics, and yet they are not swayed. We must get that approach with healing, we must base it as being based on the cross. This is the issue in a nutshell. We look around and see sickness everywhere and think this is normal. We must think of ourselves as exempt from sickness and even injury. Everything healed.

Step one is to take a look at the unbeliever when we do marketplace/street ministry. You can walk up to an unbeliever, say two words, and they are healed. On the other hand, walk up to someone who has been a Christian for fifty years and nothing happens. An unbeliever/atheist/agnostic is easier to see healed. The reason is quite simple; the majority of this people group have no concrete beliefs about healing. They haven't heard teachings on healing nor have they read all the scriptures and come to take anything as a fact. They will often remark that they do not believe a person can be instantly healed. The truth of the matter is that they haven't thought about it enough to make it an unquestionable fact. Because they have no foregone conclusion about healing, they actually have an open heart. There is no unquestionable fact (belief) that needs to be shown false and then replaced. A believer can walk up to an unbeliever, even one that is resisting, give them a quick prayer and they are healed, even if they are defiant.

I have a testimony in that regard; I was at a trailer park, well-known for being drug infested, visiting a friend. A neighbor came in talking about an upcoming back surgery. My friend started telling this man my testimony. When I simply said, "you're healed now walk", he looked at me as if I were insane. He stood there and cussed me out, then turned to leave. As he walked through the doorway, he suddenly stopped and said "what did you do to me? There is no pain". He subsequently accepted Christ on the spot.

However, with a Christian, they know all the scripture and have already reached a concrete conclusion which has formed an unquestionable fact or belief. As we are pray for them, all of their previous beliefs are bubbling up to the surface. They reject the notion even before the first word is spoken. Guess what? Even these militant Christians can be healed. Next, we get to the Christian who will state they believe and perhaps have studied divine healing being open to it. They are non-combative and very compliant and have probably seen many healings; yet, their healing has not been made substance yet.

In order to receive you must believe correctly. If I believe that Christ paid for my healing, that's a good start. It's the other type of beliefs that get in the way. If I say, " I believe Christ paid for my healing but I'm waiting on God's timing," then it's likely that person will keep on waiting. My belief that my healing is paid for is good but canceled out by a false belief. My real life example: When I was paralyzed, and diagnosed with Lou Gehrig's, I declared the Lord would heal me. That declaration was canceled out and made void because I was waiting for Him to sovereignly do it. Another example in my life was Paul's thorn in the flesh. When the disease progressed and I was put in a wheelchair, I had been told that Paul had a disease, and he had prayed three times for it to be removed. God's answer was no.

Therefore, the elders were only allowed to pray for me four times, by my own rule, and based on a false belief about Paul's thorn, I decided that God had ruled, "no" - I wouldn't be healed and therefore, I wasn't healed at that time. My belief about Paul's thorn in the flesh was completely wrong. The list goes on and on how a false belief voids out a true belief. I had started out with a correct belief, but then added false beliefs to it, which is being double-minded.

JAMES 1:6-8 (KJV)
But let him ask in faith, nothing wavering.
For he that wavereth is like a wave of the sea
driven with the wind and tossed. For let not that
man think that he shall receive anything of the Lord.
A double minded man is unstable in all his ways.

Do you see how subtle, a lie can be and how subtle being double-minded is? We look at that verse and rule out, by our own reasoning, that we are not being double-minded, yet we are. There are too many, lies of man, to deal with them one by one, it's sufficient to say that lies are slain by truth. If you need a healing and you try to rule out all of the lies of man you believe, then your healing may never happen. That is why this book started out by declaring that salvation and healing are one in the same and also why this chapter is here. The first unquestionable fact we need to have down solid is that our divine health was accomplished at the cross - period. Nothing can stop our healing, except not believing or taking it as a fact! Submit this to your heart and think about it, to the point that this truth just flows out of your mouth unexpectedly. By focusing on this truth, you negate all of the prior false beliefs. Once again, NOTHING can stop a healing EXCEPT taking as a fact that something can. If you think that you are being spiritually attacked by a demon or that the demon is blocking your healing, then guess what, you will get what you take as a fact. One last time, let's cement this into your being. Healing was accomplished at the cross and therefore the only thing that can stop our healing, is not taking that as an unquestionable fact.

How do you know when this is cemented into your heart? You're walking along doing life and suddenly a pain hits. What is your first thought; time to call a doctor? If that is your first instinct then divine health and healing is not cemented deep down. Your first instinctive reaction, shows what is in your heart. Is the first reaction, herbal remedies, pain medicine, a heating pad, or changing your diet; then that is what you are taking as fact. If your first thought is nope "In Jesus name pain go". then divine health is what you receive as a fact. On the same account, when you hear about a family member being sick, what is your instinctive reaction? "Mom get some herbal tea and put some honey in it". What are you taking as a fact? That tea and honey will provide relief? A child sprains his ankle, most of the time, the first reaction is to run and get some ice. When divine health is a fact, we declare healing first then run to get the ice.

Last year, I got a phone call from a mother, her son had broken his toe. She had immediately started declaring it to be healed. After a few minutes, she called me. and each time we declared healing the swelling and bruises went down. Within fifteen minutes, the boy was healed and running around. Her first reaction was healing which was accomplished at the cross. She would have taken him to the emergency room had it been needed. I am not saying to be stupid, but my point is that in most cases we use prayer as a secondary response. For believers, a doctor should be the secondary response.

I was driving along one day and out of the corner of my eye I saw a vehicle. The car was on the shoulder of the road and a person was in the passenger seat convulsing. Quickly, I pulled my car over and started to speak life over him. The driver was a young lady who asked if she should call an ambulance, and while still declaring healing, I shook my head yes. Within minutes, the man had recovered, thank You Jesus. The ambulance showed up and the paramedic suggested that he go to the hospital. The man was hesitant, but I told him to go and get checked out. That is how to responsibly react. My primary(first) response is Jesus; my secondary response is the medical field.

Two weeks ago, I was at a car dealership and heard a huge crash with tires squealing. There had been a wreck and all of us at the dealership started running towards the wreck. I immediately started to declare life, even as I was running. When we arrived at the vehicle it was flipped over on the hood, and was a mass of twisted steel. The man had crawled out of the vehicle somehow and was completely fine except for a cut on the arm. Thank You Jesus! In reality, he should not have survived! Everyone there was amazed that he had lived, let alone standing there talking. Most of them chalked it up to luck, chance, coincidence, but we know It was Jesus! When we take, as a fact, that divine health and healing was already accomplished at the cross, these are some examples of how we will do life. I can almost see you shaking your head and saying, "Tony, that's just you, you're special, you're anointed." Might I say in reply, "You are as well." You have the Holy Spirit, therefore you are as fully anointed as I am. The only difference is what I take as an unquestionable fact! Coffee Time!

HEBREWS 11:1 (KJV)
Now faith is the substance of things hoped for,
the evidence of things not seen.

This little verse packs a big punch. Let's unravel it just a bit. Faith is seen, hope is unseen. Hope is confidently expecting; that is scriptural Hope. It isn't wishful thinking. We have faith as the substance of things confidently expected, the evidence of things not seen. Where does our confident expectation come from? We get what we are expecting and therefore we "expect" from what we believe. What we expect to happen is formed from what we place in our self as an unquestionable fact and this applies to all areas of life. We've covered that our foundational belief should be that divine health and healing was accomplished at the cross, but now let's get more specific. If we are presently sick or become sick, how does our belief come into action.

MARK 9:23 (KJV)
Jesus said unto him, if thou canst believe,
all things are possible
to him that believeth.

Mark 5:36b (KJV)
Be not afraid, only believe

MARK 11:23 (KJV)
For verily I say unto you, That whosoever
shall say unto this mountain, Be thou removed
and be thou cast into the sea; AND SHALL NOT
DOUBT IN HIS HEART, but shall BELIEVE that
those things WHICH HE SAITH SHALL COME TO PASS;
he shall have whatsoever HE SAITH.

When our foundational belief is the accomplishment of the cross, our healing is already accomplished and then we can speak without doubt or fear and it is done already. Notice also, Jesus put this in our control with the words of our mouth, "He shall have whatsoever he says." This can be good or bad. If we keep saying that we have cancer and we're going to die, it is likely we will. That is why the foundation must be "it's already accomplished." Then, we will speak life! An example in myself is that during my sickness I kept speaking death. I looked up Lou Gehrig's disease on the internet and believed that I was a dead man and even spoke that. The more I spoke it the quicker I spiraled down. On the other hand, my wife spoke only life over me repeatedly. This counteracted what I was speaking to a point and it kept me alive, for a period of time. Remember this, ultimately, what a person believes will win out. Often we will hear in the news that a person has cancer and yet their focus is on seeing a child graduate. They will vow to live until the child graduates and most of the time they will survive until then. Although, within a few weeks after the child graduates they die. If only people were to take as a fact that they are healed!

We profess to believe that Christ is our Healer and that He is still in the healing business although, oftentimes that belief is left at the door. When a bad diagnosis occur, or when a pain hits suddenly or any other symptom occurs, in comes the enemy of God - the brain. We start relying on our physical senses as the gauge. Often, people really do take as a fact that God is our healer but still become slaves to our senses (what we see in the physical world.) Another person (doctor) tells us we are dying and we believe them, and actually take it as a fact. Then, we start speaking it out by telling everyone and we will get what we say, when we believe it. The point is this: it is easy to believe in something, i.e. a person comes to us with a diagnosis, and we believe them.

Let's take a moment to see how easy it is to take something as a fact. Your spouse calls up and says "meet me at Wal-Mart at noon." and you say okay. You drive there and your spouse is there. You took it as a fact that your spouse would be there. There was no proof or evidence that they would be there beforehand. This is "expectation" that they would be there made into a substance/evidence of your trust in them. If you hadn't gone to meet them, then your lack of trust in them would have been evidence and substance.

HEBREWS 11:1 (KJV)
Now Faith is the substance of things hoped for
The evidence of things not seen.

Do you now see how it all ties in together? You believe or take as a fact that God does occasionally heal. What do you believe about it? It just happens because it's written in the books of God. How about that Tony Myers would be healed on July 4th 2012? Jesus said otherwise, He said that when you speak to the mountain and tell it to move, then it will. If you are waiting for the date of your miracle, then that is expectation (hope) put off.

PROVERBS 13:12 (KJV)
Hope deferred maketh the heart sick:
but when the desire cometh,
it is a tree of life.

This conveniently leads us right into the next chapter where we'll be discussing HOPE and how very important it is. Let's grab us some freshly roasted coffee and gather up your thoughts. Healing shouldn't be a step by step process. It should be simply believe, expect and receive. Yet, because of the amount of wrong beliefs and teachings, oftentimes it does turn out to be step-by-step.

7 EAGER ANTICIPATION

We left off talking about hope that is deferred and I'd like to share some examples of this from my life. When diagnosed with Lou Gehrig's, my response was that the Lord Jesus would heal me and yet nothing happened. One reason was that while I was believing this to be true, I really had no HOPE or expectation. My expectation was believing that someday He would heal me and that is expectation deferred. Another time, in the back of the church, suddenly the thought came to me saying "You're healed get up and walk" and immediately another thought came that said, "Idiot you're paralyzed, you can't". Again, this was because I had no expectation. This happened three or four times and I subsequently lost all expectation and gave up. After that, I tried to kill myself, however, on July 4th everything changed in seconds. The vision that I received of Christ gave me hope/expectation. This was not a conscious thought, it was something that happened in my heart and It was at this point, that I want to encourage you. Remember, this was after six years of pure hell and now, I am able to teach from this experience in order for others to receive their miracle. The Lord is faithful to give us what we need, we just have to put forth the effort to recognize it. Don't think that my case was special or that He chose me and just a few others. That isn't the truth at all, He wants us all healed and spreading the Gospel and having a correct belief in this area is the start.

Healing is already done and nothing can stop it, except not believing that you are healed. This powerful statement in itself creates hope when it is truly taken as an unquestionable fact into your being. Hope is expectation, hope is not wishful thinking.

ROMANS 8:24 (KJV)
For we are saved by hope [expectation]:

We are saved by expectation. For now, I am using only part of this verse for a reason but we will get to the rest of it at the end of the chapter. Whenever you see the word hope, change it to expectation. This will help to change how you look at the word hope.

ROMANS 12:12 (KJV)
Rejoicing in hope [expectation];

You are expecting a pay raise, you are rejoicing in anticipation. You are planning what will happen with an increase in funds. You are expecting to be married, you are planning for a blissful life. You are expecting a child, you are planning to raise a child, and you are rejoicing. When we are expecting good things to happen, we rejoice and plan. That is why HOPE is a crucial part to receiving our healing. When we are expecting to be healed, we are rejoicing and planning. That is the nature of expectation. There are not enough words to describe the importance of expecting of The Lord. Hope/Expectation in the Lord automatically creates a lifting of the spirit! What follows are some scriptures showing a number of things about hope.

PSALM 38:15 (KJV)
For in thee, O Lord, do I hope [expect]: thou wilt hear,
O Lord my God

PSALM 33:18 (KJV)
Behold, the eye of the Lord is upon them
that fear him, upon them that hope [expect] in his mercy;

PSALM 31:24 (KJV)
Be of good courage, and he shall strengthen
your heart, all ye that hope [expect] in the Lord.

ROMANS 5:5 (KJV)
And hope [expectation] maketh not ashamed;
because the love of God is shed abroad
in our hearts by the Holy Ghost
which is given unto us.

PSALM 33:22 (KJV)
Let thy mercy, O Lord, be upon us,
according as we hope [expect] in thee.

Do you see how this changes the meaning of scripture and uplifts our spirit? When our expectation is in the Lord, He delivers. Even more so, when we know that He has already delivered our divine health to us at the cross. It is always there, always available and never disappoints. When we truly have this in our heart, then we are rejoicing and planning.

Do you believe God heals; then the answer will be yes. Do you expect to be healed, then the answer will be yes and the thousands of Christians that I pray for will all answer the same. Who is your hope in? Oh my hope (wishful thinking) is in the Lord. I hope (wishes) that He heals me. Folks, I've been there, done that, got twelve t-shirts! This isn't a put down to anyone, this is Tony speaking from experience. We have thousands of things that we take as fact and many of them are a contradiction. "The Lord is my healer but sometimes, for unknown reasons, He doesn't heal". "The Lord is my healer, why won't He heal me?" There's a Christian song out currently that says "My faith is in you, God. But when you don't part the water, I so need you to, I still have faith in you." That isn't faith, it is a contradiction. There are so many cute little sayings that show where and who our expectation is, but most of the time it isn't In Christ and His finished work. We do truly get what we expect, good or bad; ugly or awesome. We can either be slaves of our physical senses or enslave our physical senses. It comes down to if we walk in the spirit or by our physical senses.

ROMANS 8:5-8 (KJV)
For they that are after the flesh do mind
the things of the flesh; but they that are
after the Spirit the things of the Spirit.
For to be carnally minded is death; but
to be spiritually minded is life and peace.
Because the carnal mind is enmity against
God: for it is not subject to the law of God,
neither indeed can be. So then they that are
in the flesh cannot please God.

Yes, yes, yes, I know that right now your mind is focused on sin, but hopefully not, for the word flesh can be substituted, physical senses. Walking in the flesh, is more properly defined, as walking by our physical senses and this is a huge factor in determining what we are in expectation for. Using sin as an example, "why do we commit a sin?" We commit any sin because we are paying attention to our physical senses. We are walking after our physical senses. Why does anyone get tempted to commit adultery? It is by our sight; or our physical senses overwhelming us and then we give in. Name any sin and there will be a physical sense that accompanies it.

Let's take anger, we hear or see something that we don't like, and we lash out. As believers, we don't walk in the lusts of the physical senses. We are to put our physical senses in subjection to our spirit, because to live by our physical senses is death. This applies both "spiritually" and physically. If we live by our physical senses, then our choice is to respond in a physical manner. If we are angered at a person then we respond by yelling, screaming or worse, with violence. If we are coveting something that we don't have, then we respond in a physical manner by attaining that object at all cost. When walking carnally, we will reach a solution through our physical actions. Focusing on our physical senses, requires a solution through our physical senses and this is not pleasing to God. One could also say sin is a focus on a lust of the senses. Sin is in the lust of the heart, however actions often follow. The sin is in the lust, not in the action.

The same applies to sickness, for instance, our physical senses tell us something is wrong with our body. Perhaps, a doctor tells you that your cholesterol level is high; the physical reaction is medicating and possibly a diet change. Our expectation is now obviously in the carnal realm. We expect something to be done, physically speaking. We are expecting a pill or a diet change to rectify the situation, (I AM NOT SUGGESTING THAT YOU DO NOT LISTEN TO YOUR DOCTOR.) and now you are taking that physical problem and using a physical solution. An apple a day keeps the doctor away. This phrase tells us that if you want to stay healthy, eat an apple every day. Where is the focus? Eventually, the apple will let us down and we become sick. To rely or trust on the physical, is death! To rely on our physical senses is death!

Now, walking in the Spirit is life and peace (Rom 8:6). Walking in the Spirit can be accomplished while on earth, it is not being mystic, spooky, or weird. Jesus, the apostles and Paul were none of those things. I am not referring to hyper-spiritualism here, I am talking about a renewed mind that interacts with the physical world, putting the physical senses in a secondary position. While we do interact with the physical world, using our physical senses, we are not subject to them. We do not believe everything that they are telling us. We have a higher truth that we are to base our decisions upon. Let's use an anger scenario: My wife tells me something (hearing), and this causes fear to well up and anger to flow out. Now, a carnal-minded action is to react with anger, taking as an unquestionable fact that I heard her correctly. At this point, I am expecting a huge argument, and that is what happens. On the other hand, with a spiritually-minded person: My wife tells me something and I do not take what I heard from her as a fact. Therefore, no fear or expectation of an argument wells up. I speak out what I heard, saying, "This is what I'm hearing you say." These are two completely different scenarios. In the first one, I heard incorrectly and conflict arises. The second scenario; I reacted correctly and the situation ends in peace. While walking in the Spirit, there is peace and life and we see that fear never entered the situation and resolution occurred. All of this can happen because there was no taking my physical senses as an unquestionable fact. My Hope/expectation wasn't in a reliance upon my physical senses, therefore worse case reactions never happened. How about the adultery issue? A women walks up to me and starts flirting with me, but because I am not reliant on using my eyesight to reflect on her outer beauty, I never realize that she has been flirting. I was carrying on a normal conversation with her even while her motives may not have been pure. No temptation, therefore no problem in these cases, because, I take my thoughts captive and focus on what is above and not on the things of this world. My expectation is not in temptation. This is a simplification of life issues, but it is to make a great point.

We also look at "spiritual things" as being separate from the physical world. Spiritual things tend to be futuristic; "When I get to heaven" type of scenarios. When in fact, all things came from our Creator, Who is a Spirit. The physical world was brought about by the spiritual world. Therefore, the spiritual is the greater truth and is greater than the physical world. The spiritual can exist on its own without a physical world. Yet, the physical world cannot exist outside of the spiritual world. The greater spiritual truth then exists without dependence upon the physical senses, however, the physical senses are dependent upon the Spiritual Truth. It is the spiritual truth that created the physical senses, therefore they are in subject to the spiritual truth. The truth, taken as an unquestionable fact, becomes that which is confidently expected to happen. In the examples of walking in the Spirit, to be spiritually-minded includes physical health. Just as I was not tempted by a beautiful woman, because I am not focused on what my eyes take in, the same can be true for the body. When recognizing the greater spiritual truth, many things do not occur, because there is no expectation of them occurring. For instance, a weird discoloration of a mole; I see it, however, because Christ paid for and made my divine health a reality, within days it suddenly disappears. I do not get into fear or expectation of the worst case scenario and the greater truth won out. How many times has this happened in your life? Nearly every person has had a physical "scare" at some time in their life. You may have even gone to a doctor and all the tests come back normal. That is Christ's finished work in action, although we often rationalize this and mark it up as a coincidence. It is not! It is a direct result of Jesus. What we are expecting, hinges on what we believe/ take as an unquestionable fact. Good or bad, the belief that is the stronger, wins. In other words, in the case of contradictory beliefs, the one that is an unquestionable fact is the one that wins. If one says that they believe in healing, they believe that they are healed and yet, they are still sick according to the symptoms. How do we distinguish between a heart belief and what we think?

MATTHEW 12:34b (KJV)
for out of the abundance of the heart
the mouth speaketh.

Millions of people walk around saying, "I believe." Do we really? A self-check on our heart beliefs is through what naturally comes out of our mouth, when we aren't trying to speak correctly. When a person doesn't know anything about me and we are in a conversation, what they truly are expecting to happen comes out of their mouths. Once they find out who I am, they start guarding their tongue and start speaking what they consider to be correct speech. The conversation will start out like this: "I'm going to the doctor tomorrow. My test results are in and I know they are going to say, I have cancer. Hopefully, they can cure it." then when I give my testimony it turns to "Oh yes brother Tony, God is my healer. By His stripes I am healed. You know that God can heal me! Praise Jesus, He's my healer!" They've already told me a couple of things, it's the doctor that is their healer, they're expecting to have cancer and they've already diagnosed themselves. Their heart belief is in the physical world, they are walking according to the physical, not the spiritual truth. What we truly expect to happen, just naturally flows out of the mouth and that is what will happen.

PROVERBS 18:21 (KJV)
Death and life are in the power
of the tongue: and they that love
it shall eat the fruit thereof.

We speak from what is in our heart, therefore if we are constantly speaking death, this is exactly what we get. Here's the thing, simply changing the surface level won't affect anything. The surface level, in this case, are the words we speak. Simply changing our words or catching ourselves and forcing ourselves to change the words we speak, is ineffective.

Our core belief has to be what changes, and in order for that to be accomplished, we must renew our mind. Renewing our mind is to change our thought process. In changing the way we think, we then change our heart belief, that is when we will truly start speaking LIFE and healing occurs.

JOB 3:25 (KJV)
For the thing which I greatly feared
is come upon me, and that which I was
afraid of is come unto me.

We get what we expect and Job is a great biblical example of this principle. He is also a great example of showing that when there is a heart change everything can transform in an instant. Where our focus is, that is what we receive. All of this may seem a bit daunting at first. How in the world, can we change a life filled with wrong beliefs? Let me share an encouraging moment. All of this CAN change in an instant and I am living proof, all forty three years of wrong beliefs, changed instantly! Then through seeking God's Kingdom, the truths that sparked my healing became cemented into my inner being. Our Father is so good, it takes just a glimpse of truth for healing to occur. He is continually putting things in our path to give us that one spark. That spark then ignites a fire. One sentence that you've have read could spark that roaring fire. How quickly this happens is your choice. Realizing that we do indeed have a choice, empowers us.

What others hope/expect to happen, can affect us for the good or bad. Expectation can rub off, unknown to us. A scenario; when I pray for a person, based on the premise that I believe, for a fact, that our healing is already accomplished, I am expecting the person to be healed. Therefore, I am looking for a sign of improvement in that person. It is already accomplished, therefore improvement has to unquestionably happen. When I recognize an improvement, I point it out, and now that person, without conscience thought, is expecting more to happen. This is done without a long theological discussion. The person doesn't even know what I believe and doesn't have to. Recognizing that the person's voice is stronger, and pointing it out, it say "I hear your voice is stronger, are you in less pain?" They take a moment and say "why yes the pain has decreased" and my expectation has just "rubbed off" onto that person. They are then able to acknowledge that the pain is less. Then, to increase their expectation even more, I will say "Do you see what is happening? You were in a lot of pain and now you aren't. The Lord has healed you! Thank You Jesus!" The end result is that they walk away healed and encouraged. My expectation can "rub off" onto the other person. I got what I expected to happen, the other person then starts expecting the same thing. Then they are able to recognize and acknowledge their healing.

Bad case scenario: A person goes to the doctor, due to symptoms. That person is already expecting the worst, most of the time. A doctor, whose job it is to look at all the possibilities, makes a statement that we need to run some tests. They rule-out the minor issues and then orders blood work. The blood work comes back, showing the numbers are off and now the doctor is expecting cancer. The Doctor, having a good bedside manner, will often state "we will need to run more tests." That doctor, regardless of the words, is expecting cancer. The patient, picks up on this at lightning speed, and becomes fearful and now, they are also expecting cancer. This plays out in real-life to varying degrees, depending upon a person's personality and beliefs. Another scenario: A doctor reading a report, now this doctor sees hundreds of patients a year and the majority have cancer. To one degree or another, they are expecting to see positive results. As much as they try to remain objective, to a certain degree, they expect the worse and oftentimes they get what they expect to see. Now, if a believer with a renewed mind hears a bad report, and they recognize that the report was concluded on the basis of the one reading the report's expectation, whose report will you believe? This is how we can counter a bad report and have expectation in the Lord. It is a matter of either spiritual truth perspective or physical truth perspective.

The difference is, which is the greater truth and which perspective is the unquestionable fact fueling your expectation? Let's go back to Romans 8:24.

ROMANS 8:24 (KJV)
For we are saved by hope:
but hope that is seen is not hope:
for what a man seeth, why doth he yet hope for?

ROMANS 8:24 (TV)
For we are saved by expectation:
but expectation that is seen is not
expectation: for what a man sees,
why does he yet expect it.

We are saved by our expectation, yet it isn't made seen. We can know that we are in expectation by our actions. An expectant mother doesn't literally see her child, and yet she is preparing for the arrival. This is so real, she feels the baby kick, she sees the weight she's put on. There are reasons that she is confidently expecting the birth of her baby. The closer to the nine month mark she gets, the more signs she sees, that tells the baby is near. Then the birth comes and her expectation of a child in her arms becomes evident, and substance. Throughout the whole process, signs are used to point to the baby's progress. With a physical pregnancy we cannot speed-up the process. In Hebrews, we see the progress of Abraham's expectation, twenty-five years of it, and Moses' progression of expectation, Sara's as well. Some of the promises weren't fulfilled in their lifetime, such as the promised Messiah, however two thousand years ago, the promised Messiah came. Therefore, the substance, and evidence arrived two thousand years ago, so now we no longer have to make the substance a waiting game. Our Salvation and all the promises have arrived in Christ and when we believe that we have received, we have it!

8 EVIDENCE OF TRUST

Multi-faceted Faith. Let's keep it simple. Faith is simply, Trust. We tend to make things so complicated, which is why we miss the mark. Where it concerns healing, we dissect each occurrence of healing and out of those dissections we then develop certain theologies. These in turn lead to a ton of confusion and is a precursor to the trash teachings of men. Through the "trash teachings" we have then created numerous methodologies. These are methods on how to get something, that we have perceived we don't have. We teach Faith, as something to get, to grow, and to be earned.

The word faith has been used to condemn, and judge the sick, which in essence has turned many people away from believing in healing. In my own case, this was true when two weeks before my healing, the preacher looks at me and states: "You aren't healed, because you lack faith" which of course caused anger. After all, I had been the one that declared the Lord would heal me. The problem is this, we throw the word faith around without showing how trust becomes evidence and substance. We put the cart before the horse.

HEBREWS 11:1-3 (KJV)
Now faith is the substance of things hoped [expected] for,
the evidence of things not seen.
Through faith we understand that the worlds were framed
by the word of God, so that things which are seen
were not made of things that do appear.

53

By trust, we have the greater truth that all things come from the spiritual world. What appears in the world, is created by what we expect to happen, based on our beliefs (Quantum Physics). God, our Father, spoke and the world was created. Our Father spoke and put man in control of the world. The Father having put dominion of the earth in man's control, then gave man the choice to rule the world by His Wisdom or by his own wisdom. The wisdom of man is trust in the physical nature of things, based on what we understand through our physical senses. This leads us to, the physical nature of the world, which is DEATH. Adam made the choice by eating from the tree of the knowledge of good and evil. In this, we became subject to the physical world, but the coming of Christ changed that. Now, we have the choice again in Christ, through TRUST we can rule through spirit once again. The substance shows where our trust is, and the substance and evidence that is subsequently manifested is the result of our belief and who our expectation is in. We either see the evidence of life or death, the spiritual or the physical.

1 CORINTHIANS 2:5 (KJV)
That your faith [Trust] should not stand in the
wisdom of men, but in the power of God.

We tend to criticize and judge Adam; I mean how could he have made the wrong choice thereby enslaving all of mankind? Yet, In Christ we have this same choice; we can either choose life or death every day. We can choose man's wisdom or God's wisdom; the choice is entirely ours, yet we continually choose man's wisdom. We want to have increased faith in God, yet in order to do that we must start with changing our beliefs and what we take as fact, all day long! I've had to admit, at the time of my healing, I had no trust nn God. You may ask, "Then what changed?" What changed was what I believed and took as fact. Then based on a belief change, expectation was created and trust became a substance and evidence of what had been unseen. Until that moment in time, what had been seen was the evidence of death. In a single instance, even without conscience thought, a belief changed (it would seem to be almost accidentally) and trust in Christ became evident. The mistake we make is trying to gain faith/trust first without changing what we believe to be factual truth.

HEBREWS 11:6 (KJV)
But without faith it is impossible to please him:
for he that cometh to God must believe that he is,
and that he is a rewarder of them that diligently seek him.

Why?.. because without the evidence we do not have the correct belief.

How can we believe that God is the rewarder of them that seek Him while at the same time believing He sends disease? Is God pleased that we do not believe He is good? Of course not! The outcome points directly to right or wrong beliefs.

JAMES 2:22 (KJV)
Yea, a man may say, thou hast faith,
and I have works: shew me thy faith
without thy works, and I will shew thee
my faith by my works.
Seest thou how faith wrought with his works,
and by works was faith made perfect?

We are talking about the works of the Spirit, not the works of the Law. I want you to picture me climbing up a tree, getting to a branch and crawling on that branch. I am going "out on a limb". We have the faith that we need, each one of us and the reason for that statement is so we will quit thinking that we lack anything we need to be healed. We have the faith of Christ, because the Holy Spirit resides within us, Who is the Spirit of faith. Let's stop questioning that and with this solidly in our hearts, we will start seeing healing for ourselves and others. Knowing that it is a gift of God, keeps us from boasting in ourselves. Some of the following verses will make my main point.

ROMANS 12:3b (KJV)
According as God hath dealt to every man
the measure of faith.

The Father has given to every man faith! You have it.

2 CORINTHIANS 4:13 (KJV)
We having the same spirit of faith.

We've got it! We don't have to get it. When we believe we have it, then we will walk in confidence in the Lord Jesus.

GALATIONS 2:16b (KJV)
but by the faith of Jesus Christ, even we have
believed in Jesus Christ, that we might be
justified by the faith of Christ, and not by
the works of the law: for by the works of the
law shall no flesh be justified.

2 CORINTHIANS 13:5b (KJV)
Know ye not your own selves, how that
Jesus Christ is in you, except ye be reprobates?

Are you seeing it? It is the gift of the faith of Christ. Christ is in us, therefore we have His faith, the Spirit of faith, and it is a gift. How is this gift of trust/faith empowered? Through our beliefs and our confident expectation. Admittedly, faith/trust is multi-faceted. This is a starting place and will allow your confidence to grow. It is by Christ's trust in the Father that we have His righteousness and are coheirs of the promises. How do we then know if we have the correct belief? By the substance it produces. This will show where and who our trust is in and there are only two options, man or the Father.

We can recognize where our faith/trust comes from or we can run the risk of having trust in our trust or faith in our faith. I did that very thing, which is why we are discussing it. When I had made the declaration that the Lord Jesus would heal me, I actually thought that due to the declaration, my healing would occur. That is an example of having faith in my faith and not being aware that you're doing it. I had no conscience thought that this is what I was doing. Yet, many people are taught this and practice it and it can even occur in individuals who actively pray for the sick. They believe that it is their great faith that gets someone healed and they will see healings, because their belief is that the healing occurs because of their faith, however, they will be up and down and very inconsistent. That is why I keep the truth deep in my heart, that it is finished at the Cross and it is the faith/trust that is a gift from God. Then healing is no longer due to any action on my part.

Many people also believe that an "act of faith" is needed for healing. Once again, this is a form of "doing something" to get your healing. Therefore, your healing is then based on your action, not on Christ's finished work. It is unlikely that you will see results. When I pray for someone and command their healing, I will often ask them to do something. They are not asked to do this in order to get something, because I know they have it. There are two reasons for an action; to distract them and to also give them an opportunity to acknowledge improvement. The difference is what I am believing in my heart. Likewise, in my own healing, the difference between my declaration that Jesus would heal me and when I was healed, was that I wasn't moving to get it, I knew I had it. This is subtle and from the outside looking in, it would appear to be the same thing. It isn't! Let me show you through scripture.

First, those who already took their healing as a fact (believed), therefore confidently expected (hoped) to be healed, then the evidence of their trust (faith).

MARK 5:27-29 (KJV)
When she had heard of Jesus,
came in the press behind, and touched his garment.
For she said, If I may touch but his clothers,
I shall be whole. And straightway the fountain of her blood
was dried up; and she felt in her body that she
was healed of that plague.

This woman heard of Jesus, took it as a fact that if she touched his garment, then she would be healed. Her belief created expectation, which then turned into action. She was healed, before Jesus said a word. The evidence of her trust was then shown. For the centurion it was same thing, he took it as a fact that if Jesus just spoke, his servant would be healed. Jesus then states "Go thy way; and as thou hast believed, so be it done unto thee." He believed, expected, and then the evidence. Time and again, the Word shows us people who believed, expected and it happened.

For simplicity's sake, there are three types of groups when it comes to healing. Those who already believe and are confidently expecting to be healed, such as the examples above. Next you have the crowds of five thousand people, which happens over seven times in scripture. They came with the expectation of being healed. They believed, expected and received, where scripture states, ALL were healed. With Peter's shadow it was the same, it was their belief and confident expectation that produced the evidence of faith. Just as with Jesus and the woman with the issue of blood, Peter actually had little to do with it, just like with Paul's cloth. Now let's look at scripture to show where Jesus put the credit.

MATTHEW 9:22b (KJV)
Thy faith hath made thee whole.

MATTHEW 9:29b (KJV)
According to your faith be it unto you.

MATTHEW 15:28b (KJV)
O woman, great is thy faith
be it unto thee even as thou wilt.

LUKE 17:19b (KJV)
Arise, go thy way:
thy faith hath made thee whole.

MARK 9:23-24 (KJV)
Jesus said unto him, if thou
canst believe, all things are
possible to him that believeth.
And straightway the father of the
child cried out, and said with tears
Lord, I believe; help thou mine unbelief.

A few things worth mentioning on this circumstance; Jesus points to "if you can believe" or take as a fact (believe) is the starting point. There are only two cases that the desired result, didn't happen quickly. The lunatic boy, is the main focus for now. This is the only case we have a complete failure. The disciples pray for the boy, with no results, to the point that the father is questioning, whether even Jesus can heal the boy. Jesus actually, is pointing both to the disciples and to the father's unbelief. I point this out for a purpose, healing has a dual responsibility. In all the other cases what does Jesus point out, "As you believe, let it be done. Your faith has made you whole." People think, all of the responsibility lies on the one who is praying. That thinking process leads people to take no responsibility for their own healing and many miss out. At healing services, many people think brother or sister " so and so " has the power to heal alone and that is why many leave disappointed. They believe it is all up to the one person praying, in spite of their own beliefs. By the same token, at a healing service, many people are expecting and that spirit of expectation does rub off onto others and many people get healed that would not have done so in any other situation. In my own life, I have many examples of both sides; where I did believe, expect and receive and also where I did not. Depending on the circumstance, some things are more difficult to believe for, than others. The disciples had seen great numbers of people healed prior to the circumstance above. It was because of the convulsions and foaming at the mouth, that caused them to question themselves. They allowed their physical senses to supersede the unquestionable fact that Jesus had told them to heal the sick. Which then affected the believing and expectation of the boy's father. Just like the wind and waves stopped Peter from believing!

Let's skip to the third group, this is simple. They are the cessationists and they are not even around. In Jesus' hometown he could do no mighty miracles, save heal a few sick. This people group, did not go to Jesus at all.

They stayed away from Him, mocked and avoided Him. We have this group of people today. Unless, they change their belief they won't be healed, because they do not seek it. They refuse the very concept.

The second group are those who Jesus approached. They weren't coming to him and they weren't expecting to even meet Him. This is very comparable to street ministry when we approach people. Let's talk about the pool of Bethesda.

JOHN 5:6-8 (KJV)

When Jesus saw him lie, and that he had
been now a long time in that case, he saith unto
him, Wilt thou be made whole?
The impotent man answered him, Sir, I have
no man, when the water is troubled, to put me
into the pool: but while I am coming another
steppeth down before me. Jesus saith unto him,
Rise, take up thy bed, and walk.

In this case, the man is asked by Jesus. "Do you want to be healed?" The man's answer reveals where his expectation lies and therefore what his trust is in; it is in the pool of water. Jesus then does the last thing that the man expects, "Rise, take up thy bed, and walk." This throws the man's mind off-balance and he is no longer thinking, "Oh poor me, no one will carry me to the pool". While his mind is trying to grasp this, he does just as ordered. The man believed in healing, or he wouldn't have been at the pool, although he wasn't expecting it. Jesus breaks this man's focus on the physical circumstance, distracting his mind from the physical circumstances, allowing healing to happen.

JOHN 9:6-7 (KJV)

When he had thus spoken, he spat on the
ground, and made clay from the spittle, and
he anointed the eyes of the blind man, with the
clay. And said unto him, Go, wash in the pool of
Siloam, (which is by interpretation, Sent.)
He went his way therefore, and washed, and came seeing.

This example is very similar, Jesus distracted his physical senses. These aren't methods (a process to get something), it was to distract the physical senses. You will obtain whatever you are focused on, or where your expectation is. If you confuse the carnal mind (physical senses), and get them focused on something else, then they will recognize what has already been achieved. How many times have you been in pain and set your focus intently upon a task, subsequently not feeling any pain until the task is complete. Think about it! You can be working very hard, completely focused on a specific task, and when the task is finished, you see blood and THEN your finger starts to hurt.

ACTS 3: 5-7 (KJV)
And he gave heed unto them, expecting to
receive something of them. Then Peter said,
Silver and gold have I none; but such as I have
give I thee: In the name of Jesus Christ of Nazareth
rise up and walk. And he took him by the right hand,
and lifted him up: and immediately
his feet and ankle bones received strength.

We can observe that this group of people had no preconceived thought or expectation of being healed, nor extreme faith. Notice that in this second group no one states that this person had any faith. When the barrier of their physical senses was removed, they were healed. The first group of people had the correct belief and they took their healing as an unquestionable fact. Because of that fact, they were expecting to be healed and as soon as they heard Jesus was close by, they had formed it as a fact in their innermost being. This resulted in their trust/faith being made substance and evidence. The third group did the exact opposite, based on a preconceived notion, they chose not to believe and therefore their expectation and trust was in their "run of the mill" everyday lives.

Can you see how these things all work together? An interjection here; I want to thank God The Father for the Holy Spirit. When we are listening, He will lead us like a horse to water, directly to our healing or if we are praying for someone's healing, He will show us where this person is and what is needed for them to acknowledge their healing! Stop trying to get the faith, that is a gift. The Gift - The Spirit of God; residing in the temple that is our body! The next chapter is the final foundational truth that fully encompasses the true believer's life and with this final piece, you are healed!

9 KRAZY THING CALLED LOVE

1 CORINTHIANS 13:13 (KJV)
And now abideth faith, hope, charity, these
three; but the greatest of these is charity.

Trust, expectation, and love are the essence of the believer's lifestyle. The greatest being love, which is what binds everything else together. This could really get dicey! This portion could cause you to lay the book down and never pick it up again, so take this with a grain of salt. Maybe you should take it with a tablespoon of salt. Go to your kitchen and ingest a whole tablespoon of salt. DO NOT LISTEN, DON'T DO IT.

Let's start with the messy part and define the old and new covenants first. Forget the salt, grab a cup of coffee instead. In simplicity, the old covenant can be defined by two simple statements. The old covenant was strictly about loving God in a servant to master relationship. Love was a one-way street, being commanded to love God, without love reciprocated. The old covenant focused only on the physical senses of man. It only focused on the physical things of this physical world. Through the law of Moses, God was teaching mankind about the spiritual, through the things of the physical world. Do not mistake me, the Father loves His creation and in fact, it was this very point that the Jewish leaders missed. They took what was handed down by Moses and it became all commands without love. They even added to it, so there would be no chance of stepping across the line. The commandments were written in stone, cold, hard stone, with no power. Yet, even within the old covenant, the ones who saw past the commands and entered into relationship with God, experienced His love. David, Moses, the prophets, the mighty men of God, all saw past the commands and experienced God's love. The religious leaders saw only the physical laws, with physical practices and did not experience the love, behind those laws.

MATTHEW 23:23 (KJV)
Woe unto you, scribes and Pharisees, hypocrites!
For ye pay tithe of mint and anise and cummin
and have omitted the weightier matters of the law,
judgment, mercy, and faith: these ought ye to have
done, and not to leave the other undone.

Judgment is assessing a situation, or one could say it's discernment, and Jesus gave many examples. When He healed on the Sabbath, Jesus was showing the Pharisees the Father's heart. The example of David eating the shewbread, is another example and yet these leaders saw only the commands and not the love beyond the commands. God gave the physical commands to show what love looks like. However, when only viewing the physical law without assessment, mercy, and trust, it becomes harsh, cruel, binding and restrictive. Without love, it is captivity.

A real life example is this, I visit a former "crack house" for a bible study. The woman who lives there is newly baptized and has just accepted Christ. A religious person passing by sees me there, and in their eyes I am now addicted to drugs and a hypocrite. They have JUDGED me guilty, instead of assessing the situation from the eyes of discernment (seeing the bible in my hand), mercy (giving me the benefit of the doubt), and trust (assuming, I had a legitimate reason to be there). Instead, they automatically assume the worst.

I also visit a bar, and a person that only sees the physical laws automatically assumes that I am there getting drunk. In their eyes I am "backslidden". They see my car in the parking lot and judge me as a drunk. There is no discernment, mercy or trust. A person who is "religious" is looking for a law of God to be broken and therefore even when the situation doesn't concern them, they feel it is their moral obligation to pass judgment. Whereas, a person in relationship with the Father, in the new covenant, wouldn't even think twice and probably wouldn't even recognize my car in the parking lot. Love expects the best, and the law is looking for a trespass.

Oh no! You've got me started. One day, I was sitting in the bar witnessing to an individual. I had a plate of food in front of me and a cup of coffee. A fellow came in, a perfect stranger, peaked inside and then left. A few minutes later, I walked out the door, walked to my car. This same person came up to me and said he was pastor so-and-so, and that he was calling the cops, because he wasn't going to allow a drunk to drive. Oh my gosh!! I could have just said, "Okay, call them." I owed that man no explanation and I could have stood there, waited on the cops and let him get embarrassed. Instead, I explained to him that I was simply having lunch and witnessing to a person (I actually love their food, awesome pizza!). He continued to inform me that a Christian should not be in a bar and that I was going to hell. That is the modern version of a person living under the law. There was no discernment, mercy, or trust in a situation that was none of his business to begin with, and in short, no love.

That is one aspect of the old covenant, the other aspect is in the physical things being used to show the spiritual. Oil in the old covenant is used to represent the Holy Spirit. Food is used to represent clean and unclean and tithing is used to represent giving. The temple is used to represent God's dwelling place and the list goes on. These are physical representations of the spiritual. An old covenant mindset doesn't move past the physical, into the spiritual. An old covenant mindset is so focused on the physical, that the physical is all they see. There is no love, only objects. Oil is still a representation of the Holy Spirit, without recognizing that the Holy Spirit, the real oil, has come into the world and was poured out on all flesh. This mindset will still see the church as being a holy dwelling place of God without recognizing that we are now God's temple. Food will still be a representation of either being clean or unclean, being godly or ungodly, not recognizing the spiritual Bread has come. In this old covenant way of thinking, tithing must be to a specific place with a specific amount attached, not recognizing that we should simply give abundantly to those in need. An old covenant mindset, is restricting, unbending, unyielding and only sees the physical form. There is no love, involved. Therefore, without Love being God's essence, how can a person be healed when the focus is only the physical nature. If we are only looking at physical things and judging them either broken or whole, how can one understand a body being broken down one minute and made completely whole the next?

The physical healing of a body will also lead to the spiritual, however within the rigors of an old covenant mindset, that focuses only on the physical aspects, a physical healing cannot be embraced. I ask then, how can that person truly believe in the spiritual salvation? If I do not believe in a loving God that wants His physical temple completely healthy, that which can be seen; then how can we believe that through Christ our sins are forgiven, which is unseen? If I can't believe that with a few words a paralyzed body can suddenly move, when that is seen; how can I believe in eternal salvation, when I don't see the end result, until death? Ponder on this and really think about it. An example would be, Jesus first tells the paralytic man "your sins are forgiven thee"; then He tells the Pharisees "which is easier, to say, your sins are forgiven or get up and walk?" He was using the physical healing to show the spiritual, but the old covenant mindset cannot grasp this reality. Enter into the new covenant mindset which because of Love, can grasp and understand both the physical and spiritual, because the physical is housed within the spiritual, and it is LOVE!

The new covenant is a completely different mindset than the old covenant. The new covenant starts with the Father's love for us. Our righteousness is no longer as filthy rags, because our unrighteousness is traded for Christ's righteousness. We go from sinners to saints; from servants to sons. We are now His precious children, Christ was the firstborn of many. We went from looking for God's mercy, to having His mercy. No longer am I looking to cold stone to save me. I am looking straight at the love of the Father. We now have proof of how precious we are to Him. This proof is never failing and always there as a reminder.

1 JOHN 4:19 (KJV)
WE LOVE HIM, BECAUSE HE FIRST LOVED US.

JOHN 3:16 (KJV)
For God so loved the world,
that he gave his only begotten Son,
that whosoever believeth in him should
not perish, but have everlasting life.

1 JOHN 4:9 (KJV)
In this was manifested the love of God
toward us, because that God sent his only
begotten Son into the world, that we might
live through him.

The new covenant starts from the top and flows downward as the Word declares, we love Him, because He first Loved us. What is the proof that we are valuable to Him, He sent His only begotten Son! Why do we take communion; as a reminder of Christ's Suffering? No, as a constant reminder of the Father's love for us. Christ was resurrected, He is not suffering anymore. What then is the point of remembering Christ's body and blood? Why did Christ say, "do this in remembrance of Me?"; as a reminder of how much the Father and Son love us. The Father sowed His Son, so that we could become son's. The Son, Jesus, chose to give His life for us. That, my friends is how much He loves us and we don't need any further proof than that. This is the reason we take communion, it is a reminder of how precious we are. It is that very love that we are to share with others. With this in mind, now that we are His temple, we carry the glory of Christ within us and how could we think that the Father's will is for us to be sick? An old covenant mindset believes we are worthless, and cannot believe in the love of Father God; therefore, we stay sick and needlessly I might add. Let's look at some more scriptures. Your mind may be screaming at me right now, "But the Father poured His wrath onto His Son and therefore sickness is God's wrath towards sin!" Hold that thought, well actually don't hold it, get rid of that thought because it isn't true! Let me make a few more points and then I'll destroy that erroneous belief.

1 JOHN 4:17 (KJV)
Herein is our love made perfect,
that we may have boldness in the day
of judgment: because as he is,
SO ARE WE IN THIS WORLD.

Did Jesus ever get sick prior to the Cross? No, He did not, and so then after the cross, since we are "as He is now in this world," why should we get sick? Can you imagine Jesus ever being sick? He is within us, does His Holy Spirit get sick? Where is the Kingdom of God,,, within us! Therefore should we get sick? NO. Why do we get sick? It is because we believe a lie. Remember the verse above, 1 John 4:9 "that we should live through HIM." If we are living through Christ, then what applies to Him applies to us, WHEN we believe it. The old covenant, un-renewed mind, cannot believe this truth. That is the carnal mind speaking, which is at enmity towards the things of God, neither can understand the things of God. Restating, if we are to live through Christ IN US, then what applies to HIM, applies to us. If He couldn't get sick, before the Cross, then He certainly cannot get sick, now! When we believe this, then we will be healed, and we won't get sick. "Just say Uncle and believe."

Let's get back to God's wrath being poured out onto His Son, because how can we believe that God wants us healthy, if He'd pour out His Wrath onto the perfect sibling. Would an earthly parent, discipline the perfect child? So then with this teaching, God allowed, not only allowed, but poured His Wrath onto His Only Begotten Son. How can it stand to reason that sickness isn't within God's will? Let's do some explaining, once again, starting in the garden of Eden. By one man, Adam, death entered the world through sin. By ONE MAN, the second Adam, Jesus, the original sin and death was escorted out of the world. God gave man dominion over the world, and He never rescinded that order; therefore, Jesus had to come as a man and take the world out of darkness. There are two things operating the Kingdom of light and this kingdom speaks only life. God's Kingdom rules this earth. The cross wasn't God pouring out His wrath onto Jesus, as is taught; it was Jesus accepting sin into His body, thereby trapping sin. Then, when He gave His life, Jesus took sin out of this world. Jesus took two types of sin, the original sin of Adam and the sins of the children of Israel under the law of Moses; thus fulfilling not destroying the old covenant which was fulfilled and replaced by the new covenant. In order for us to be partakers of this covenant, we must believe that Jesus was resurrected from the dead, thereby replacing death with LIFE. Since death and it's causes came through the original sin, these were taken into Christ along with the sin. With that explanation in mind, note that God did not forsake Christ at the cross nor turn His back on Him or pour out His wrath onto Him. These three points will be covered, but know this, the loving Father did not turn His back on Christ.

PSALM 22: 23-24 (KJV)
Ye that fear the Lord, praise him; all ye
seed of Jacob, glorify Him; and fear Him, all
ye the seed of Israel. For He hath not despised nor
abhorred the affliction of the afflicted, neither hath
He hid his face from Him; but when He cried unto Him
He heard.

This psalm is all about Christ, which starts out with "My God, My God why hast Thou forsaken Me?" We have been taught that the Father turned His back on the Son, yet He didn't. Jesus speaks out "My God, My God" because He was referencing this entire psalm specifically, not saying that the Father had abandoned Him. Jesus accepted sin into His body, but the judgment wasn't against Jesus, neither was it wrath. Rather, it was sin being condemned along with everything associated with sin including the causes of death. The bronze serpent holds the answer:

NUMBERS 21:8 (KJV)
And the LORD said unto Moses,
Make thee a fiery serpent, and set it
upon a pole: and it shall come to pass,
that every one that is bitten,
when he looks upon it, shall live.

The fiery serpent (sin) is a representation of Jesus becoming sin on the cross as cursed is every man that hangs upon a tree. When the children of Israel looked upon the fiery serpent, they saw what was killing them (being cursed or put to death.) and they lived. It is the same thing with us, we look upon Jesus and see that which had been killing us being put to death within Jesus' body and we live when we acknowledge, His finished work! Note that the annual sacrificial lamb, which again represents Christ, the lamb's throat was slit, there was no wrath involved there. Isaac, becoming a sacrifice, yet there was no wrath involved. In every representation of the shadow of things to come, there was no wrath involved. Jesus became sin. Sin was not poured into Him by the Father. In fact, the judgment wasn't against Christ at all, it was against the sin that His flesh had taken on, and this is what was put to death. For instance, if one wants to contain something, let's say bacteria, you cannot contain it with something that is of the same nature as the bacteria. In order to keep it contained, it has to be held by something that is not contaminated by the bacteria. That is why Christ had to be perfect and was perfect. There was no contamination within Christ's body, therefore He alone could contain the sin of Adam and Israel. This enabled Christ to put sin to death and return to LIFE uninfected! There is no wrath involved in that process.

JOHN 12:32 (KJV)
And I, if I be lifted up from the earth,
will draw all men unto me.

JOHN 12:32 (TV)
And I, if I be lifted up, will draw all sin/judgment unto me
(like a lightening rod)!

In context, the above is the better interpretation. Most translations use men, or everyone. Based off of verse twenty-one this is incorrect. In which Jesus states, The time for judging this world is come, when satan the ruler of this world will be cast out. Satan is cast out by Jesus taking sin upon Himself. No wrath from The Father is involved in this. Did Jesus ever state that His Father would pour out wrath upon him? No, instead He told us who God's wrath would be poured out on.

MATTHEW 21:37-39 (KJV)
But last of all He sent unto them His Son,
They will reverence My Son. But when the
husbandmen saw the Son, they said among
themselves, This is the Heir; come, let us kill Him,
and let us seize on His inheritance. And they caught Him,

and cast Him out of the vineyard, and slew Him.
Then Jesus asked "what will the lord do to them?"

Their response was that He would destroy the wicked men. Where is the wrath of the Father? Upon the one's that slew His Son, not on the Son.

MATTHEW 21: 45 (KJV)
And when the chief priests and Pharisees
had heard His parables, they perceived that He spake of them.

The Father's wrath was not poured out on the cross to Jesus, in fact all of Matthew 23 shows Jesus is condemning the chief priests and Pharisees. I hope you can see the Father's love in all of this. I have heard people say that God sent His Son to die. God the Father did not condemn Jesus to death the Pharisees, priests, and scribes did. Time and again, we hear people try to credit the Father for the evil of men. Yet, in His great mercy, the Father sent the Son, knowing the outcome and we see in this verse:

ISAIAH 53:10 (KJV)
Yet it pleased the Lord to bruise him;
He hath put Him to grief: when thou
shalt make His soul an offering for sin,
He shall see His seed, He shall prolong His days,
and the pleasure of the Lord shall prosper in His hand.

This isn't the Father saying that He was the one who bruised Jesus; this is the Father taking responsibility for sending Him in the flesh so that we would be saved. The pleasure of the Lord was the eventual end outcome; many sons and the restoration of His creation so that we can now be sons of God. When that becomes a deep down revelation made real, then we can understand our Father's love and then we can believe that it is His will for us to be healed now! The whole struggle in life is coming to the revelation of the Father's true personality, which is pure unadulterated love. The more revelation we have of this fact, the more we can reflect the Father's true nature. Before I get all mushy, and lovey-dovey, let me share one more point. Who crucified Christ? Who put Christ to death? Many will say, God through man or that God's wrath toward man had to be poured out onto Christ. Now, sin had to be punished, so who put Christ to death?

1 CORINTHIANS 2:8 (KJV)
Which none of the princes of this world knew:
for had they known it, they would not have

crucified the Lord of glory.

There's the answer, it was the princes of this world and they had the choice.

ROMANS 2:4 (KJV)
Or despisest thou the riches of his goodness
and forbearance and longsuffering;
not knowintg that the goodness
of God leadeth thee to repentence?

It is the goodness of the Lord that changes our mind about His nature.

ROMANS 11:22 (KJV)
Behold therefore the goodness and severity of God:
on them which fell severity:
but toward thee, goodness, if thou continue in His goodness:
otherwise thou also shalt be cut off.

Continue in His goodness, know His nature and then we can continue in His nature. You may be asking yourself "Why, in a book about healing, have we discussed all of this?" Because it all comes down to the love of the Father.

2 TIMOTHY 2:15 (KJV)
Study to shew thyself approved unto God,
a workman that needeth not to be ashamed,
RIGHTLY DIVIDING THE WORD OF TRUTH.

The Father does not have two natures; good and evil. Rightly dividing the word of truth, is separating God's Nature (GOOD) from man's nature (Evil). We will receive from the side (good or bad) that we are believing from and the Father isn't duality in nature, man is. We either have the mind of Christ or the carnal mind, good or evil, we don't want a mixture. If we think that God is good and bad we get a mixture. God created Adam in His image, which showed only goodness. God then walked with Adam, but what happened was that Adam ate the fruit and that changed him, not God. Therefore sin and death entered the world, but not through God's judgment it was by Adam's action. Everything that speaks LIFE is of God and everything that speaks death is of man. Christ restored us and now we can have a choice to make. Choose this day LIFE or DEATH........choose LIFE!

Love is what will spark the fire to choose life, because then we have the Father's nature and we're empowered in Christ. With that empowerment, there is no disease that can touch us. Indeed, there is no disease or impairment that can stay within our body. We have the choice, always and every moment of the day, to choose life. Knowing the full nature of Christ empowers us to live from that nature in our own bodies and then love gives us the authority to drive it out of other's bodies. While we are striving to fully mature in Christ, this appears to be circumstantial. In each set of circumstances we have the choice, life or death. Until we achieve the fullness of Christ, if I notice a pain in my body, then I have a choice. I can listen to the physical senses that speak death to me or I can choose the mind of Christ and the Holy Spirit which speaks only life. Knowing His love prepares us for this because love is the deciding factor.

Love, "correctly believing", "confidently expecting" and then seeing the evidence and substance is all you need to know to receive what Jesus' body paid for, and you can give this knowledge to others to show what the truth of the good news is all about. Many of you have come to this truth with open hearts. You were healed somewhere between the start of this book to where we are now. Then there are others who are still skeptical. You have a million questions or should I say "buts", such as "But Tony that all sounds too easy." "But Tony, the devil walks around like a roaring lion", "But Tony, the thief comes to steal, kill, and destroy", "But Tony it ain't that simple".

I should end the book right here BUT I know people and want to see you healed. Keep on reading and perhaps some of your "buts" will get answered. Let me re-phrase and completely change that. Most of you have no clue how to walk this thing out. I've taught and told you what to believe and now you need to see how it all plays out. The next chapter deals with this being walked out for yourself, then for family members, then for others. Time to get the ole' coffee maker working and get this moving along.

10 WALKING HEALING OUT

Most of you should know by now that both my Christian and healing journey started on July 4th, 2012. Grab my book, The Lord Jesus Healed Me, for the full testimony of Jesus. Yet, my healing journey hasn't stopped there concerning both myself and others. In this chapter, we will be dealing with "walking out healing for yourself" and what this should look like.

JAMES 4:7 (KJV)
Submit yourselves therefore to God.
Resist the devil, and he will flee from you.

Okay, you now believe in divine health and that you are a son of God and yet, you are still sick. Everything in our life that is bad, you guessed it, it's from the devil. It doesn't matter if it is a cancer, paralysis from a broken neck or a cold, it is demonic and it is not from God. Let's talk through a brief scenario: A thief is in your house, and you say, "I've got a gun, stop!" We will say this with authority, "You're in my house, stop or die!" Our belief is that the thief has to stop and we're not expecting anything less. Resisting the devil and all his works is no different. Another scenario: We have a 6 year old child whom we tell to go and clean his room. We say this to them as an unquestionable fact. "Go clean your room." We confidently expect it to happen and it happens, and there we have our trust/faith in the child made into evidence and proof. It is no different with whatever issue we are going through. We now know that it was finished at the cross, the Father loves us. This means it has to go, so resist, in your own words tell it to go, out loud.

When speaking to a thief or a child we don't softly speak in our mind or thoughts. We speak it out loud! This is what we expect to happen, now do it! Then we are looking for the results. If it was pain, we acknowledge that the pain has subsided or decreased. In the case of an unmovable limb, we expect to be able to move it. With cancer, we expect the numbers to be normal at the next blood test. With a lump, expect it to be less noticeable or better yet, completely gone. Based on who we are in Christ, we are not looking for the symptom, we are looking for the healing and we accept nothing less. That is resisting the devil! There are no examples of Jesus asking God for His will to be done, because He already knew what the Father's will is. By now, we should know as well, that His will was already accomplished at the Cross. We are now sons of God and should be living like it. When we believe what we're saying, when it is a fact to us, then it is done. We can then forget about it and move on.

The severe stomach pain that I spoke about earlier in the book, for a time, during that prior night, I wasn't resisting the devil. My physical pain overpowered my resister. The next morning, a conscience decision was made to resist and I started praising the Lord and then the healing happened. With my eyesight, I was having to wear glasses, bifocals by the way, with no resistance against the devil. Finally, I made the decision to resist. This healing did not happen overnight, but instead it took roughly a month for my eyes to be completely healed. It was not that God delayed my healing, it was me needing the time to come to the FACT that I was healed. There are some things that are harder to believe that we are healed than others.

When I say "resisting the devil", I don't mean you need to yell, scream, or beat your chest, or even include him in the conversation. All I have to know is that Jesus already paid for whatever is coming against my body. There are times, it may be helpful, to say no outloud. If it doesn't appear to be progressing forward, I re-visit the love of the Father and Jesus. I re-focus on the fact that I am already healed and I expect to see improvement. This is what I did until my eyesight was completely restored and that was over four years ago. Some days I saw improvement immediately, other days not so much. Meanwhile, the whole time I was studying the word and renewing my mind. Then one day, my dog ate my glasses, yes literally! I rejected the lie that I needed to wear them anymore and then both my near and far vision cleared up.

That was early on in my journey and I hadn't put into my heart, set in concrete, that divine health is already mine. The deeper that revelation gets, the less physical things happen. Then when something does happen, we already have the truth, and we can overcome. One key is to not look for something to happen. We can't get into the mindset of, "I was healed from that, now I'm waiting for the next problem to arise." We have to get into the mind-set of divine health; "I am the temple of the Holy Spirit therefore no sickness can come upon me." I don't live from sickness to sickness, instead I go from the standpoint that I already have divine health. When something does happen, I do not get into condemnation. I'm not looking for a reason why I am being attacked. My thought has become, "Is the Holy Spirit within me, sick? - NO, Then neither am I." Maybe it was the taco I ate last night? Nope, food doesn't have an impact on Jesus' health so it doesn't affect mine either. This is not conforming to the physical world, I am within the BODY of Christ. I am in the physical world, but not conformed or dependent upon it.

Several years ago, a mysterious pain hit my leg. This pain cut right through my bone and when anything brushed against it, the pain would hit deep. I was being a little bit casual about it, simply telling it to go, but It got worse. One day, my wife touched the spot and I jumped about five feet into the air. That did it, she was on me QUICK. Have you prayed over it? "Yes", I answered. "Have you asked anyone else to pray over it?" she asked. "No", I answered. She kept on telling me to get a ministry friend to pray for it and I finally did after two months. When they prayed for me (commanding it to go), it would leave. Then, as soon as we hung the phone up, it would come right back. After about another month of this, I was sitting down just refreshing my memory on all that I've seen and been healed from. I was reviewing my beliefs, starting off with the fact that Jesus paid for my divine health and therefore this had to go. Then, meditating on the verse "when you pray (declare) believing that you HAVE received, then you shall have it." The proof is in the pudding and the bottom line was that I was trying to get something that I already had. I pondered this verse for roughly an hour and within that period of time, it left never to return.

As you can see, each scenario is different and the healing comes about in different ways. Yet, what is always the same is my foundation, it is already done, I have it, I'm not trying to get it. I take this as a fact and then I expect change and results. My actions are always different, on the outside my response looks different, but I am not using my physical senses as the gauge to whether "it works". It already worked two thousand years ago.

Some things that I don't do: ignore the pain, deny the symptoms, lie, nor do I look for the pain. I do acknowledge the symptoms, something is wrong, and it doesn't belong in my body. I'm not "bravely" denying the symptoms. The truth overcomes the reality of my body. I do not get into fear because fear is a lack of trust. We are not given the spirit of fear, but of a sound mind. When I say "I am healed", if it sounds like a lie, it is a lie. Deep down we can tell if it sounds like a lie or the truth. When the spiritual truth overshadows the physical reality, then I will state "I am healed" and it is the truth whether the symptoms are there or not and then the symptoms will leave. When something happens, I recognize that I am healed. Then I will move, or otherwise take notice, not of the symptoms but on the improvement from them. The question isn't "Is the pain still there?" It is, "What is the level of pain, did it decrease?" That is where my hope, my expectation comes in. I am looking for improvement and I go with my first reaction. My first reaction will, most likely, be truth and the response after that will be rationalizing. "Yes, it went down, Thank You Jesus." I get excited about any improvement and so should you. Praise the Lord! If there is no improvement, I am still healed and that is still the truth. I am simply not recognizing where the improvement is. If there is no improvement, then I change my focus. I will distract myself. I will do something that takes my full attention away from the symptoms. Then while doing that, at some point, do a quick check expecting it to be gone, looking for improvement. We often miss out on what we have (healing), because we are concentrating on what we perceive is unchanged. Instead of noticing the slight decrease in pain level, we feel a little bit of pain and that becomes "I'm still in pain, it didn't work."

Healing for ourselves is difficult, because we are feeling the symptoms. It is not an indicator that there is a lack. Do not beat yourself up. I've been there and heard all the thoughts; "What is wrong with me? I've seen so many people healed, yet the "healer", can't heal himself." Don't even go there. "I lack faith", don't go there either. I've already shown you that we have the faith, it's built inside of us, because Holy Spirit is there. Just strive to make the revelation that we have divine health now, because of the cross and renew your mind to the fact that it is your physical senses lying to you. Use any means available to increase your expectation, testimonies are a great way of doing this and always look for improvement, expecting improvement and grabbing a hold of any slight improvement! Be completely honest with yourself. If you're in fear, admit to it, speak it out, recognize it, and then speak the exact opposite. "I'm in fear, but the Lord did not give me a spirit of fear, but a sound mind". Recognizing the lie and exposing it breaks its back. The father of the lunatic boy, did this, "I believe, help my unbelief."

Don't hear a testimony and try to reconstruct what worked for them.

That is when healing becomes a method, trying to get something you feel you don't have, it won't work. Believe, expect, and see results. My testimonies are mine, yours are yours. We are healed because we took it as a fact we were healed, expected improvement, and the substance and evidence then became apparent. Every time, every case, every circumstance. If there are crazy laid out steps to follow, then it is wrong(see Chapter 4). You may have "tried and tried" to be healed without results, that is why the body of Christ is here, we are to pray for one to another. ~ Coffee, and time for the next chapter.

11 THE BODY OF CHRIST

Oh my friend, you just turned the wrong page, to the wrong chapter and just stepped right onto my pet peeve! Well, that is better than saying you just stepped into my pet's dung. This chapter is going to start with showing you how you can pray for the sick and see them healed, and if you are reading this book, you can, should, and will. After that, we will get into how to go about it. If you are sick and have tried to get healing for yourself and haven't seen the lying symptoms leave, grab a fellow believer (that correctly believes) and get them to pray for you. That's what this thing called a "Believer's Life" is all about. We are the body of Christ, and when one part isn't functioning, the others should jump in. You don't have to travel ten thousand, gazillion miles or find a certain person. If I get sarcastic during this part, have some mercy on me. Many people aren't healed because they are looking for the "right" person with the "right" anointing to get them healed. We will go from "anointed" healer to "anointed" healer and never find healing. In the past and present, and future leadership in the church has misrepresented healing and the other "gifts". Please, my friend, never ever call me an "anointed healer". You will not like me very much after my response if you do; especially, if I know you've read this book!

EPHESIANS 4: 7 (KJV)
But unto every one of us is given
grace according to the gift of Christ
And he gave some, apostles; and some,
prophets; and some, evangelists; and some

pastors and teachers; For the perfecting of
the saints, for the work of the ministry
for the edifying of the body of Christ:

Everyone of us is given empowerment/grace, according to the fullness of Christ. The leadership of the body of Christ is there to equip the saints for the work of the ministry. The five-fold ministry is there to teach believers to walk in their truest identity. We are ALL empowered with the Holy Spirit. HE is the gift given to every believer. You may point to the scripture that states the gifts, and say, "Nope, Tony you're wrong you have the gift of healing." WRONG! Look up that scripture in the Strong's concordance and you will not find the meaning of the word gift there. I am not going to get all Greeky on you here. It's true that there are some, who from constant use, are better equipped than others, but we all have the full measure of Christ in us. Instead of going through the semantics in-depth, proving to you this truth, I am going to get you to use some sense, that ain't common.

ACTS 10:38 (KJV)
How God anointed Jesus of Nazareth
with the Holy Ghost and with power:
who went about doing good, and healing
all that were oppressed of the devil,
for God was with him.

What is the anointing? Anointing means, poured out or upon. God "poured upon" Jesus the Holy Spirit and power. In the day of Pentecost, God poured out His Spirit (God is the Holy Spirit) upon all flesh. Now, with the baptism, which simply means "immersed", of The Holy Spirit, we are all empowered to operate in all the ways of the Holy Spirit. We are all told to heal the sick and furthermore in the gospels, every single disciple was part of healing the sick and casting out devils. After the twelve, there was the seventy and then the additional two that weren't even a part of Jesus' group. In fact, Jesus sent them all out before Him into the cities, healing the sick, before He even arrived. Jesus wasn't a one-man show, He actually empowered all that were around Him to do the same. He also said, "greater things than these you will do." Good leadership will set the example for all to follow. If healing were accomplished at the cross, then guess what, there is no personal glory in it for me. When I see someone healed, it was already accomplished by Christ at the Cross. If I am to be great in the Kingdom of God, then I should be the least. Therefore, it doesn't matter how many people I see healed. If twelve people read this book and all twelve people start praying for the sick, then I have equipped others. I have then played my part in God's Kingdom. This book isn't about convincing you to do it, this book is about getting you healed and giving that away to others. In your daily lives, as you go about your daily routine, share what you've been freely given, the gift of the Holy Spirit. Just a few verses to show that healing is for all believers In Christ.

MARK 16:17-18 (KJV)
And these signs shall follow them that believe;
In my name shall they cast out devils; they shall
speak with new tongues; they shall take up serpents;
and if they drink any deadly thing it shall not hurt them;
they shall lay hands on the sick, and they shall recover.

"Them that believe", includes every single believer not just a few. As we live out our daily lives, we should be ministering to others. My goal is to help make healing so readily available to everyone that there are zero sick believers. Then, all those believers will be ministering to unbelievers, to the degree that there is no more sickness. A lofty goal you might say, well YES!, but with God all things are possible!

You are already equipped and are doing this out of love. You believe, expect (Hope) and then the evidence manifests in another person's body. You take it as a fact that Christ accomplished divine health as much for the other person as for yourself. The method is the cross and resurrection of Jesus, therefore, there is no pressure on yourself or the other person. It is already accomplished, so no brow-beating, blaming or accusing. We aren't trying to prove anything to the other person. We are simply showing them how much the Father and Jesus loves them and that He made healing available to all.

Right now, I'm talking about what is commonly referred to as marketplace ministry, or simply healing others as I go about my daily life. Since every person is different, there is no set approach. This is casual, no pressure whatsoever. As easily as we give a cashier money, ask for directions or simply say hello to a perfect stranger; that is how we approach people. Very casually, there doesn't have to be any bravado.

While standing in line at McDonald's, behind me was a woman, who had one of those big post-surgery boots on. I just started talking about the weather, how mild the winter had been. She tells me that she just had surgery and the pain she's in. I then comment, "Well, In Jesus name the pain is gone". Then I simply ask, "How is the pain?" She gets this gorgeous smile and says "it's gone." Then I share my testimony with her, because it's a long line. We talk about Jesus, and I find out that she is a Christian, so I simply say, "if you notice pain later on, just tell it to go away." Then I order my food. Simple, easy, no bravado, no pre-rehearsed script or one-two-three steps. If you want to literally follow the command to "lay hands", then just stick your hand out, they'll grab it and if they don't grab it, that's fine don't let it worry you.

I was at a car dealership, as part of my business, waiting to speak to a manager. An older fellow's arm was in a sling. He was looking at the showroom car. I asked him, "What in the world did you do to your shoulder?" He responded, that his rotator cuff was messed up. I gave him my testimony, and then said "Move it, how does it feel?" He moved it around still in the sling, and said, "Wow, the pain is gone!" He took the sling off and said "Thank You Jesus." Turned out, the other shoulder was messed up as well and this time I said, "Shoulder be healed", he moved it without even my telling him to. Thank You Jesus! These are snapshots of how normal this can be.

If a person is in an extreme hurry or acting fidgety, that's fine. I'll just casually say "Be blessed", and move on. There's no telling the number of times I've said that to someone and then all of a sudden they turn around and say, "I had tremendous back pain and it left". Thank You Jesus! Often, that will develop into a longer conversation.

Once I was eating dinner at a restaurant with a friend and I had a feeling the waitress was in pain. I simply asked her if she was in back pain. "Yes" she stated. I just said "pain leave, how is it?" "It's gone", she replies. She got super excited and ran into the back, and my friend and I heard her telling the other waitresses what had happened. Often this will lead to praying over more people.

A few cautions and a warning: If you are not doing this out of love, and wanting to see people set free from oppression, then please don't do it. If you are praying for the sick, just to attract attention or to become the next famous preacher, leave it to someone else. If you intend to pray for the sick out of duty and obligation, please step away. We are dealing with hurting people who have feelings and emotions. If you are on a power trip or for your own gain, rethink your motives and ask the Lord to change your heart attitude. Growing in maturity is one thing, but doing this without love can be damaging. We can all pray for the sick and see them healed, Christ accomplished it for us, please keep this in mind. I know too many healing evangelists and individuals who do this for their own selfish reasons and have hurt people. I could give example after example of this and also please feel free to use the words "I don't know", instead of giving an opinion. Make sure when you are asked a question that you truly have an inner witness from the Holy Spirit and are giving an appropriate response otherwise point them to a ministry like this one. Mistakes are fine, and I've made my share, so don't let me discourage you; but know where your maturity level is in this, so you can respond with love. For heaven's sake, please don't give your version of what I'm teaching, such as, "Well Tony Myers says_____." Let them hear one of my teachings or read this book for themselves, thank you very much. Okay, done with the pet peeves, let's move on.

I'm going to throw a lot of tips at you. Don't worry or give a lot of thought to possible rejection from people. More often than not, very few people will take offense, as long as you approach with genuine love. Every person is different, every situation is different and in that way, there is no formula. The Holy Spirit will, as I'm speaking, show me what to speak and do for that person. A starting point is to just say "hi" with a big ol' genuine smile. Take a few minutes to simply converse with them and most often you will gain some trust with them. At some point, ask if they would like prayer. Honestly, I don't ask, haven't for quite a while now, but that's just me. The "prayer" shouldn't be long, you aren't begging, pleading, or wishful thinking. It's already done, so anything within a half a second is good. I'm kind of joking, but the shorter the prayer the better, after all Jesus and the disciples were always very short. In fact, it was mostly "get up and walk" "go" and so on and so forth. Just find a starting point. "In Jesus name, blindness go away", "broken leg be healed". Then ask them to move and how does it feel? Simple, short, and sweet. Watch them, and if you see improvement point it out to them. Make a big deal out of it. Make a statement to give them something to think about, "Hey one minute you're in a lot of pain and now you aren't, wow thank you Jesus".

Be pleasant, introduce yourself, engage them in conversation, pray for them, ask them if they have improvement, watch them for improvement. Thank Jesus for their healing. This is a simplistic teaching, because the focus on this book, isn't marketplace ministry but I did want to give you some very basic guidelines.

Marketplace ministry is very fun and fulfilling. Remember, we're not out there to put another notch in our healing belt. We are out to give people what they so badly need, the love of Christ. Go by their cue, if they are rushed or hurried let them go, don't try to force them to listen. I don't interrupt them if they are eating dinner at a nice restaurant. I look for the opportunity to engage them on their terms, not on mine. There are times we are to be bold, absolutely. I've had some very crazy experiences, but most of the time being non-intrusive is the way to go. The majority of the time, Jesus and the disciples healed those who came to them. Do not put yourself on a quota that you need to fill or commitment to pray for ten people every day. Pray for people, as the opportunity arises.

On a Thanksgiving Day, one year, my laptop went kaput. My wife saw that there was a sale going on at Wal-Mart, so we went. It was crazy!! Our intention was simply to grab the laptop and run (after paying for the laptop, of course). We arrived an hour early as the sale was set to start at six. While waiting, I was talking to a woman in a wheelchair. I gave her my testimony, and as I was doing this, her husband walks up and lets her know that he was heading over to check something out and would be right back. After giving my testimony, I simply stated, "Get up and walk". I held out my hand, she grabbed it and stood up and walked. Thank you Jesus! Her husband returned to see his wife prancing around the aisle, and then a prayer line formed and people started asking for prayer. If memory serves me correctly, about five people in wheelchairs were healed and fifteen or so other people. That is really awesome when that happens. It is much more awesome when it spontaneously happens and not purposefully created.

Grow, mature, and share the love of Christ, as you go let the signs follow you. The more experiences you have, the more you will learn. Take the first step and it will become a lifestyle. People, at some point, will seek you out when they are in need. That will then be the opportunity to teach what you have learned. Don't pattern yourself after someone else; just be you, after all you are the temple of the Holy Spirit.

12 DEALING WITH THE FAMILY

After my healing, I started praying for the sick and I had a family member who had been just as sick as I was, whom I had tried to reach out to continually, only to get slapped in the face. As much as we want to see our family, immediate or distant, walk in health, it is their choice. My entire family knew of my healing. Many of them had seen me in a physically crippled state a mere year before, when they had come to say their farewell. Then, after I was healed, they were amazed. Yet, seldom do they ask for prayer or my advice on healing. At times, especially at first, I forced the issue and this is neither wise nor recommended. Subsequently, this chapter is on keeping the peace; ministering to family when they are accepting and when they aren't.

MATTHEW 13:57 (KJV)
And they were offended in him. But Jesus
said unto them, A prophet is not without
honour, save in his own country,
and in his own house.

The word prophet here is generalized; this can mean any one of us, not the office of a prophet. Those who know us, often will not come to us. They've seen us at our best and at our worst. We can either be a huge testimony to them or destroy that testimony, by forcing it on them. Use wisdom, offer them the choice to hear you out. Offer them the choice, but don't force the issue, even if they are on their death bed. The Father allows us to have the choice in all matters, so take His example. He doesn't force anything upon us, and it does no good to force the issue. Let them know your hand is always extended to them and how to contact you about healing.

With that stated, prayer is powerful, and yet, we need to learn how to pray to see results. In my family, whenever I find out that a person is struggling physically, I speak it out exactly as if I were there physically. There is no time, space or distance with our words, they are powerful, no matter what. The only difference is: I'm not there to point out improvement to them. Jesus, with the centurion, did the same thing by simply telling him to "let it be done as you desire." I still command the sickness to go and expect a report that the person is doing better, because once again, it is already accomplished for us. Therefore, there is no begging, pleading or wishful thinking, I expect it to happen. For prayers such as seeing people accept Christ, my wording is a bit different because Holy Spirit works through people. I will ask the Father to send a person into their life that will have an impact on them, that can touch them. All of my prayers for others are worded in this way. The Father and Jesus simply need us to command heaven to earth and knowing who we are in Christ is vital.

When a family member is open to direct prayer, often I will tell others to act as if that family member is a perfect stranger. Especially, if it is a spouse or child. Whatever room they're in, once you walk into that doorway, to pray for them, see them as a perfect stranger. Go in, pray for them, ask them how they feel and leave the room. Then re-enter the room, and they are back to being family. It is the same way when we pray for ourselves, we are personally invested in it. We've seen their symptoms, which makes it harder to overcome what our physical senses are telling us. With kids it is wise not to even ask them how they feel. Let them get distracted doing something else and observe them to see improvement. Especially with kids, even if they feel better, they will tell you they feel the same. Depending on someone's personality, a distraction is often an essential tool. Sometimes changing the conversation or saying something silly, will change their focus. Then, they will be able to then recognize improvement.

Recently my wife and I went through a six month ordeal. She was extremely ill. This was so serious, she had to be flown to a hospital which was three hours away. I spent my days, for two weeks, driving six hours a day back and forth to see her. Situations like these can develop, and this is where we know the Father's love for us. We know our healing was already accomplished, in spite of the symptoms and we take it as a fact that they are already healed. We expect to see improvement, NOW, not sometime in the future. Part of my wife's problem was a stroke, but by the time she arrived at the hospital there were no more signs of a stroke. Then there were some other things as well, which shall remain unmentioned. Let me put it this way, without a solid foundation, I would have crumbled. Sometimes, just plain old grit and determination, "perseverance", is an absolute must! Keep the amount of others you ask to pray, to a minimum; reason being that we only want life spoken over our loved ones. Many people, out of the best of intentions will speak death. A total of six people knew of my wife's situation. Contrary to popular belief, prayer boards, telling everyone you know, or starting prayer chains, is not the way to go.

Think about this, in the past two years how many famous preachers, prophets or well-known men and women of God have passed away? They had thousands of people or perhaps millions praying for them. The reason, at least in part, is due to people having wrong believes about healing. They impart these incorrect beliefs when they pray. Also, the more we tell people about our loved one being sick, the more focus there is on the sickness. We are magnifying the sickness which does not build hope/expectation, rather it destroys it. The more people involved, the more you have to repeat the diagnosis, which is not good for building up expectation and the focus then becomes on the gravity of the situation. Instead, as soon as a negative doctor's report comes back, declare life against it.

When Jesus and the disciples were healing people, how many of them did it take? It took, one person. How many people prayed for Paul when he was bitten by the snake coming out of the fire? No one, not even himself. He simply threw it in the fire and kept going. My point is simply this, have the smallest number of people involved that is possible. This is an ongoing mistake many Christians make, because they want to fire up the troops and get as many people involved as possible. This causes self-pity to spring up as well. Have a small group, four to five, like minded believers involved praying for your loved one and for your support. Choose people that will only speak healing, and life.

With that stated, I kept speaking life, my trusted friends kept speaking life. I refused to think and/or speak anything other than healing. If one of these people heard me speak anything but life, they would correct me. I kept myself to love, believe, expect, and the evidence would manifest which was my baseline foundational truth; her body wasn't the gauge. The truth was, she was healed no matter what my physical senses were telling me. Yes, there were moments of tears and thoughts of doubt. When there was doubt, I would speak it out loud and immediately speak the exact opposite. I constantly declared life, a sound mind and a healthy body. Thank you

Jesus.

Let's shift gears, and talk about a topic that is avoided. I have prayed over family members and other people that have died. It is unavoidable at this point and we will, at one time or another, see and feel the loss of life.

13 DEATH LOSING ITS STING

We have all lost at least one loved one, most of us multiple. The Father's creation is precious to Him. We are His creation and we are precious to Him. This chapter is about clearing up some misconceptions, to my understanding, at this time. Let's look at a misused verse:

1 THESSALONIANS 4:13 (KJV)
But I would not have you to be ignorant, brethren,
concerning them which are asleep, that ye
sorrow not, even as others which have no hope.

This scripture does not mean, that we cannot feel sorrow over the loss of a loved one. This doesn't mean, we can't cry, or miss them. It means what it says to not sorrow as those who have no hope. We have the expectation of seeing them again. Many gentiles of that age, when a loved one died, carried on excessively, with howling, screaming; even hiring mourners to create, an overly excessive scene. Paul, is comforting them, that we will see our loved ones again. This is not a command to not feel the loss of a loved one. We see Jesus, and even Paul, weeping, and sorrowful over the loss of loved ones.

JOHN 11:34-35 (KJV)
And said, where have ye laid him? They said unto
him, Lord, come and see. Jesus wept.

Jesus wept, knowing that in a few minutes He would be raising Lazarus from the dead. This weeping shows us that it is fine and acceptable to grieve and also we see through Jesus, how the Father responds to loss of life.

Quit blaming God the Father of life for death! This is the single most blasphemous lie to ever come forth from a human being's mouth. God is love not death. God did not bring death into the world, sin did. The "cute" sayings that we use need to stop, such as "The Lord gives and takes away." or "If the Lord's will is to take me home.." and again, "I think it's time for the Lord to take me home." When we use these types of sayings, we speak against God's will not for it.

MATTHEW 18:14 (KJV)
Even so it is not the will of your Father
which is in heaven, that one of these little
ones should perish.

JOHN 10:10 (KJV)
The thief cometh not, but for to steal, kill, and to destroy
I am come that they might have life,
and that they might have it more abundantly.

LUKE 9:56 (KJV)
For the Son of man is not come to
destroy men's lives, but to save them.

It is amazing to me, that we wish to find God guilty of murder. We blame the One who told us not to kill. Is He a hypocrite that He tells us not to kill, but then He kills? Jesus who is the exact image of the Father, states that it is not the will of the Father that anyone perish. It is Job who stated, "The Lord gives and takes away", not the Lord Himself. In John 10:10, we have Jesus saying that it is the thief who steals. Is He accusing the Father in heaven of stealing? I think not! Who then comes to steal, kill and destroy? It is the thief, not our loving Father. Whose word should we listen to, and who is the authority, is it Jesus or Job? Are you going to believe Job, who even stated later in the book that he had spoken "amiss", over Jesus? Many people do and every Sunday there is a preacher somewhere on planet earth accusing God of taking lives when Jesus states the exact opposite.

JAMES 1:17 (KJV)
Every good gift and every perfect gift
is from above, and cometh down from the

Father of lights, with whom is no variableness,
neither shadow of turning.

This is James stating that there is no darkness in the Father at all. So then by this, are we calling death a good gift? Don't answer, that!

ISAIAH 5:20 (KJV)
Woe unto them that call evil good,
and good evil; that put darkness
for light, and light for darkness;
that put bitter for sweet, and sweet
for bitter!

1 JOHN 1:5 (KJV)
This then is the message which we have
heard of him, and declare unto you,
that God is light, and in Him is no
darkness at all.

This is when you point to the old testament scriptures and note that God did this and did that. Who should be the authority, your perception of old testament scriptures, or Jesus? Jesus came to reveal the Father to man, which means that all scripture needs to be viewed through Jesus, and what He says about the Father. Let's look at an old covenant prophet who got it wrong and this can be proven.

2 KINGS 1:12 (KJV)
And Elijah answered and said to the captain of fifty,
if I be a man of God then let fire come down from
heaven, and consume thee and thy fifty.
And there came down fire from heaven,
and consumed him and his fifty.

LUKE 9:53-55 (KJV)
And they did not receive him, because his
face was as though he would go to Jerusalem.
And when his disciples James and John saw this,
they said, Lord, wilt thou that we command fire
to come down from heaven, and consume them
even as Elias did? But he turned, and rebuked them,
and said, Ye know not what manner of spirit ye are of.

Now let's look at a these similar examples side-by-side, in the OT example the captain had merely told Elijah to come down and in the next NT example the Samaritans shoved, beat, and pushed the Son of God,Son of Man, Jesus.

HEBREWS 13:8 (KJV)
Jesus Christ the same yesterday, and today, and forever.

In the first scripture Jesus is the WORD of God, therefore it would have been the Word that would have made it happen, i.e. the fire consuming men. Elijah himself, was acting in the wrong manner of spirit just as Jesus rebuked John and James of doing. We must view scripture through the only reliable filter, Jesus. Can you imagine Jesus destroying or killing men? Then it isn't God who is doing the killing. God is pure love and incapable of evil. He does not repay evil for evil. The true nature of God is revealed by Jesus. Any other way, is pure foolishness. The reason for the discrepancy is that until Jesus:

1 John 5:12 (KJV)
No man hath seen God at any time;

Hold on, Moses did right? Moses saw God from the rock crevice, right? Who is wrong here? What John means, in the above scripture, is that until Jesus no one correctly knew the Father's nature. The prophets and the others had no concept of satan and they thought God was both good and evil. When satan is mentioned, it is as the angel of death, who was God's servant. Jesus shows us differently, for the first time, that there is an enemy to the Kingdom of God. There is much more and the more we learn about the Father's true nature, the more we learn He is incapable of evil. God is pure light, in Whom there is no darkness! When we make statements such as, "God, I'm ready to go home now", we are really asking satan to kill us. There is much more I could show you on this topic, however, this should suffice for now and hopefully it peaked your interest to study this out for yourself.

1 JOHN 5:20 (KJV)
And we know that the Son of God is come,
and hath given us an understanding, that we
may know him that is true, and we are in him
that is true, even in his Son Jesus Christ.
This is the true God, and eternal life.

I am going to show you another scripture that shows us blaming God, when it was really satan at fault.

2 SAMUEL 24:1 (KJV)
And again the anger of the Lord was kindled
against Israel, and he moved David against
them to say, Go, number Israel and Judah.

Reminder: it was God who told David not to number Israel. Yet, He moved David against Israel? Remember James 13? "neither tempteth He any man?" Let's see who this really was, God or satan?

1 CHRONICLES 21:1 (KJV)
And satan stood up against Israel,
and provoked David to number Israel.

Same exact incident, yet one account says it was God and one account satan, are you seeing this? God is being blamed for the works of satan! Now, we have the choice, satan cannot just take our life. He doesn't have that kind of authority. He can however deceive us into giving our life up. How does he accomplish that? Through hopelessness, lack of expectation, and desire and yes, he can also influence those under his control to take lives. If we are living under his influence, he can get people to make the choice to get drunk and thereby kill another person. All of the means of loss of life, murder and suicide are satan working through people. Yes, he must always work through people, but even in these cases, I do believe in one way or another, we have a choice based on our personal revelation of God's goodness and how protected we are prior to these circumstances. The better we know the true nature of God, the more protected we are. The more of His love we walk in, the more protected we are.

Jesus is my favorite example of this very thing. Many times, the Pharisees sought to kill Him and He would walk right through them. Who knew the love of the Father better than Jesus, no one! There was nothing that could touch Jesus, no disease or man-laid plans that could touch Jesus, until He gave himself up. Paul was the same way, with the number of times he should have been dead, yet he survived even more torturous things than Jesus. Jesus was only scourged once, Paul was inflicted this way five times. Paul was finally martyred, when he gave himself up. Paul was himself raised from the dead often. Here is my point, to the extent that we know the Father's true nature which is love, to this extent we are protected and in this way, we choose life or death every day. Even at the cross, Jesus had the choice, and states this himself.

MATTHEW 26:53 (KJV)
Thinkest thou that I cannot now pray to my Father,
and he shall presently give me more than
twelve legions of angels?

Christ is the first born of many and in Him, we are as He is, in this world, and yes, we do have the choice. You may fire back at me, "What about with children, how can they have a choice?" I have no firm response to this question, so I will tell you straight up, I don't know. However, I will state that we do get what we expect. If a parent truly believes in heart, that his (her) child is protected, then he is.

EPHESIANS 6:16 (KJV)
Above all, taking the shield of faith,
wherewith ye shall be able to quench
all the fiery darts of the wicked.

The Father is always good, and never, ever has any involvement with evil. He is always ready to intervene and will. He needs our cooperation, which is what we are growing and maturing into. We need to have the correct belief, confidently expecting, in His goodness, then the substance will manifest and become evidence. Many times, we fail to acknowledge when there was divine intervention on our behalf. We chalk it up to circumstances or chance. Martyrdom and dying to oneself, is often glamorized. An in depth teaching on these misconceptions, would take another book to explain. Suffice it to say, Jesus sacrificed His life so we don't have to. Killing the flesh is not living with disease and in poverty. If an earthly father, wanted a child to live like that, we would call it child abuse. That isn't Our Heavenly Father's nature either.

Let's go from death due to outside circumstances, to death by disease or old age. We must always remember that the Father never forces His will upon us; it is always our choice. As a man thinks in his heart, so is he. Healing doesn't just drop out of the sky. I can't wave a magic wand and boom - that person is healed. I can however, speak life, then it is up to the other person to acknowledge life. Healing is always available and quite frequently it happens instantaneously. We have to want it for ourselves, no one including Jesus, can force anything upon another person that they don't want. If the Father Himself or Jesus, can't force Their will upon another, neither can satan, or demons.

The realm of darkness cannot force death to come, but rather death comes, when we give up. This is huge and the body of Christ needs to come to this understanding. When we start teaching this truth, people will start fulfilling God's will and life on earth won't end by disease, it will end peacefully when that person's purpose is fully completed. Many people die before their purpose is fulfilled and that is a tragedy. I firmly believe that people can and do die for Christ's name sake. Jesus did, Paul did, and the other disciples did as well. This was brought about by man, in the realm of darkness; literally speaking, I am talking about disease. In God's kingdom, this does not have to be. Society views disease as normal and inevitable; that disease will strike and we are almost helpless to do anything about it. Our expectation is put into one area, medicine. If the doctors can't combat it, then we're doomed! This is a problem, because we give up and think we are powerless. We seem to think that when death comes knocking we have to open the door. This is a huge topic with a lot of misconceptions. For now, let me scripturally prove how only we can give up our life. Why do we give up our life, because we lose all expectation. We get crushed down by pain, lack of mobility, loneliness, suffering and tragedy and then we give up the ghost. We feel powerless and make the decision consciously or otherwise, to give up the ghost. We have numerous, example of this.

GENESIS 25:8 (KJV)
Then Abraham gave up the ghost,

GENESIS 35:29 (KJV)
And Isaac gave up the ghost, and died,

GENESIS 49:33
And when Jacob.....
and yielded up the ghost,

MATTHEW 27:50 (KJV)
Jesus, when he had cried again with a loud
voice, yielded up the ghost.

ACTS 5:10 (KJV)
Then fell she down straightway
at his feet, and yielded up the ghost:

ACTS 5:5 (KJV)
And Ananias hearing these words fell down,
and gave up the ghost:

PROVERBS 17:22 (KJV)

A merry heart doeth good like a medicine:
but a broken spirit drieth the bones.

A person that has suffered for a long period of time, gives up the expectation, of living. We see this time again, in nursing homes, and in hospitals. They give up the desire to live, and that is their choice to make.

PROVERBS 13:12 (KJV)
Hope deferred, maketh the heart sick:
but when the desire cometh,
it is the tree of life.

Each one of us, is empowered to make the choice.

DEUTERONOMY 30:19 (KJV)
I call heaven and earth to record
this day against you, that I have
set before you life and death,
blessing and cursing: therefore
choose life, that both thou and thy seed may live:

PROVERBS 18:21 (KJV)
Death and life are in the power of the tongue:
and they that love it shall eat the fruit thereof.

The major problem is most of us do choose death over life. Once we believe that the Father has given us the choice, we then make decisions based on that choice. There is empowerment in this truth! The individual always has a choice, whether that person knows it or not. We say that God makes the decision, but He says in His word that He gave us the choice. This book is really about showing that we do have the choice. We can make the decision to walk in perfect health, because of Christ. We have the choice and the more the body of Christ believes this, the more we will walk in it. We will come to the full stature of Christ, when as a BODY in unity, we come to speak only life.

Ultimately, it is a person's choice to be healed or not. While we are on the subject of death, let's talk about resurrecting the dead.

MATTHEW 22:32 (KJV)
I am the God of Abraham,
and the God of Isaac,
and the God of Jacob?

God is not the God of the dead,
but of the living.

Many people turn from the Father because a loved one dies. People also turn away from divine healing because a loved one dies. Hopefully, we are now seeing that it is a choice. When praying for a loved one to be resurrected, that also is the choice of that person. When a person leaves their body, they are alive, not dead. Therefore, when I command a person to be resurrected, God gives them the choice, and He doesn't see them as dead. As the above scripture states, He is not the God of the dead, but the living. Therefore, our loved one has the final word. This is my opinion, but I ask you, if we are in heaven, as we perceive it to be, how many of us would choose to leave the ultimate paradise? There are only two reasons that I can recognize; if that person is in hell, or if a purpose on earth is unfulfilled and that purpose is tantamount! That purpose is so huge, that it overshadows the desire to be in paradise. I have discussed this matter with some who have been raised from the dead. The majority of people, that I've spoken to have agreed. I am really proposing this as "food for thought".

14 DEFEATED REALM OF EVIL

We were talking about choices, and there are only two, the Holy Spirit and life or the realm of darkness and death. Every day, we make a commitment to one or the other, there is no third option. Peter was being praised one moment, having a revelation that only the Father could have given to him, that Christ was the Messiah. Then Peter turned around and misspoke and Jesus rebuked him, because he had embraced a lie from satan. The middle ground doesn't exist. We are either working life from the Holy Spirit or death from the father of lies. As sons and daughters of the living Father, we have the choice, in Christ. We as people love to categorize and label things and in this chapter we're going to do two things: declassify two categories and unify them. Then we will put the devil and his minions in their respective places- defeated!.

We have a tendency to split healing and deliverance into 2 different categories, but Jesus didn't. In fact, He didn't divide any ministry. He ministered salvation to all, who wanted it. Salvation meaning the fullness of our Father. Salvation is healed, saved, delivered, set free and made whole. There should not be a prophetic ministry, deliverance ministry, healing ministry etc.., because we all have the anointing, which is the Holy Spirit. Each disciple walked in every aspect of ministry. Now, I can respect those who operate in separate ministries, but I am just stating that there will come a day when Christianity recognizes the truth of what I just said. Jesus told the disciples to go out there and heal the sick, raise the dead, cast out devils, he never separated the disciples at any time. We don't see Jesus saying, "ok you three deliver, you three heal, you three raise the dead.." It was an all-in-one command to everyone. The five-fold offices are there to equip the saints for ministry, not to have separate ministries.

With that stated, the single source of all evil is the realm of darkness. Whether we perceive the evil to be a "natural disease", or demonically influenced is irrelevant, it is all demonic. Nothing evil is "naturally" how God created it. In ministering, if it isn't of God then we tell it to go. Mental illness, evil spirits, disease, all of these things are trying to do one thing, exalt itself over the authority of Christ. It is exalting itself over the true reality of the victory attained at the cross. And exalting itself by imaginations against the knowledge God gives us about our authority in Christ. Here's the simple truth, deliverance is no different than healing. When we love, believe, and expect; then the substance and evidence manifests.

2 CORINTHIANS 11:3 (KJV)
But I fear, lest by any means,
as the serpent beguiled Eve through his
subtilty, so your minds should be corrupted
from the simplicity that is Christ.

We, as carnal-minded men, make up all these rules that Christ never demonstrated. As far as deliverance goes, as in everything, there are the two extremes. The first mindset is that we as Christians don't need to concern ourselves with deliverance and that if demons do exist, they cannot bother us. First off, what is a demon, it is a lie in which the carrier is an unseen spiritual being. Its sole purpose is to get you to grab a hold of that lie. We can recognize it by what it carries. Spirit of anger, depression, so on and so forth. It is my belief that if we are unaware, then yes, a believer can certainly grab onto and believe that lie. Peter is a good example of this.

MATTHEW 16:22-23 (KJV)
Then Peter took him, and began to rebuke him,
saying, Be it far from thee, Lord: this shall not be
unto thee. But he turned, and said unto Peter,
Get thee behind me, Satan: thou art an offence
unto me: for thou savourest not the things that be
of God, but those that be of men.

John and James are another example, when they wished to call fire down from heaven. In both instances, Jesus simply addressed the lie and broke it.

Now, especially with unbelievers, it can get much worse. The lie can become the reality in which that spirit takes absolute control over the person. When I was an atheist, I had many examples of this. This is why Paul tells us to take our thoughts captive. We still have partial control, which depends on each person, which thoughts they grab onto and to what level they take it. Many of my actions of insanity, if not all, were demonic. I would cut myself, hurt others, attempt suicide, think thoughts of taking my vehicle and smashing it into a building to kill people. Actually, one time I did run my car into the house where I was living. By God's mercy alone, no one was injured. I also had severe PTSD, and was diagnosed as being a schizoid (denoting or having a personality type characterized by emotional aloofness and solitary habits) By my own experience, this is confirmation that demons do exist, but let's not think of them as all powerful beings with limitless power. Don't go into sci-fi mode on me.

The other side is exactly opposite, we mistakenly think they are all powerful and we will have to have a long battle to get delivered. Some think there are demons everywhere and if you don't be careful, they can take you over almost at will and make you slither like a snake, howl at the moon. Or the thought that says, "Don't touch anyone, or they can give you a demon." Yes, there are both sides. I've known Christians that do think like this, but having been, demon possessed, I tell you, they can't make you do anything you don't want to do. Essentially, what happens is, you constantly think these insane thoughts and then eventually you act on them. Demons are powerless unless we give them a place. Demons have to work through man, flesh and blood. A person has to accept them and even an atheist has a certain amount of control. Can a person go completely over to insanity, yes if we allow it, by our thoughts. The man in the tombs is proof that we do have control. He was unsaved and demonized, yet he ran to Jesus. The demon wasn't running to Jesus, it was the man running to Jesus.

MARK 5:6 (KJV)
But when he saw Jesus afar off, he ran and worshipped him,

The meat of this conversation, the truth of Jesus is in the middle. Remember that casting out a demon is no different than a disease, the source of evil is the same. Therefore, the solution is the same, Jesus! Love, believe, expect and the substance will be evidenced. Too many in the deliverance ministry treat demons as if they are so powerful and it is such a fight. We have all seen videos of people having convulsions and manifesting. A deliverance minister will tell you that is normal and that the demon is fighting. Then we get the idea that demons are so powerful they can block a healing, and you have to cast them out first. We think that some demons are more powerful than others and can fight for days months and years. These things happen because we in our hearts are expecting these things to happen. Because of the cross, all are defeated there is no listing of one demon being more powerful than another. They are defeated. If a boxer is knocked-out, he's defeated. Does he have any power? No. We are giving a defeated realm power they don't have. Our focus is on defeated foe, when it should be seeking God's Kingdom. Many people are demonized, solely because they believe that they can be. Many people are in spiritual warfare, battling unseen foes because they think they have to battle. The focus is then on the realm of darkness, not on God's Kingdom and this is wrong.

The common thought is that we are fighting disembodied creatures and so we struggle against them and they manifest in physical ways, forcing people to do things against their will. We can't see them, so we think they can enter our bodies at will and then we have to do their bidding. We then get these cute little sayings like "another level, a stronger devil". Young Christians are being told, "When you accept Christ, be prepared, the devil is going to attack you." We use our imaginations, and get a misperception of the power of the realm of darkness. Demons, no matter what manner we choose to picture them, are simply, vessels that carry lies. The only power they contain is within the lie that they carry. The only struggle we have is to believe the lie or the truth.

JOHN 6:63 (KJV)
It is the spirit that quickeneth; the flesh profiteth
nothing: the words that I speak unto you,
they are spirit, and they are life.

Words are spirit, therefore Jesus' words were spirit and life. The exact opposite therefore is also true; a man's words can be spirit and death. Therefore our words are bouncing around the atmosphere waiting to be accepted or rejected. If this is true, then what mountainous struggle can they give us?

A deliverance minister bases a successful deliverance on their physical senses and this brings us right around to the scope of this book. We walk by faith/trust not by sight. There are deliverance ministries teaching that if you burp, fart, cry etc. then a spirit is leaving. They teach that demons come in through the orifices of the body, thereby saying that they also have to leave that way, with physical evidence of that exit. Lies do enter by our physical senses, but they are gone when that lie is destroyed, with no need for physical evidence. Lies enter when we believe the physical senses over the spiritual truth. Demons, when exposed, are simply destroyed and no physical evidence is required. The evidence comes from the proof of freedom in a person's life. These misperceptions can cause theologies to be birthed that are just ridiculous. I have been in deliverance classes where a person will say, "I just burped, so I'm delivered". Yet, their life shows no true freedom. According to this practice, the same person has farted out a hundred demons, yet still prone to irrational anger. How many farts does it take to be free? I make light of this, but it is a serious matter. Let's get the truth out there, quit magnifying the devil. "The devil is resisting, still there, I'm not delivered" are common words coming from many that want to be delivered. You resist the devil and he will flee. Scripture never says the devil can resist you. All of these misconceptions are based from a scripture that is not understood. We have the authority in Christ to cast out lies, no matter what vessel they are transported by. Don't accept the lie. I respect the deliverance ministry, yet let's not stay in the same place. Let's move forward into a fuller view of the truth.

Deliverance is freedom, living in true freedom in Christ. We attain freedom by accepting truth. There is nothing that can withstand truth, except not believing truth. I've given you a scope of what I was like while demonized and it was worse than I described. I had nightmares, flashbacks and much more. Yet, on July 4th 2012, all of this was instantly vanquished. There was no struggle. Who better for demons to attack then a person who had never read the Bible? Thank You Father and Jesus, I hadn't been told that there was supposed to be an epic battle!

EPHESIANS 6:12 (KJV)
For we wrestle not against flesh and blood,
but against principalities, against powers,
against the rulers of the darkness of this
world, against spiritual wickedness in high places.

This scripture is talking about that we are wrestling against, the spirits that the leaders of this world choose to embrace. Our weapon is Christ and truth. Mention that words spiritual warfare and the image we have is the creatures known as demons, attacking us and we have to keep quoting scripture and hollering "I pour the blood of Christ on me and you can't attack me." We're shouting at the air.

EPHESIANS 6:11 (KJV)
Put on the whole armour of God,
that ye may be able to stand against
the wiles of the devil.

What is the armour of God: truth, righteousness, peace, salvation, the Word of God, and faith. Put on Christ in us. The wiles of the devil, are simply believing lies. What is the solution? Paul tells us.

2 CORINTHIANS 10:3-5 (KJV)
For though we walk in the flesh
we do not war after the flesh:
(For the weapons of our warfare
are not carnal, but mighty through
God to the pulling down of strongholds;)

The solution is drum roll please.....

Casting down imaginations, and every
high thing that exalteth itself
against the knowledge of God,
and bringing into captivity every
thought to the obedience of Christ;

ROMANS 12:2 (KJV)
And be not conformed to this world:
but be ye transformed by the renewing
of your mind, that ye may prove what
is that good, and acceptable, perfect, will of God.

There are demons, yes, don't get the idea that I don't believe there are. I have cast them out of many people. Can a Christian get a demon, well sure, they can accept lies. Dispel the lie with the truth and it is done. Cast it out of your mind. With others, we have the authority to cast out demons and then they have to renew their mind to the truth. Many times, I've been told that a spirit keeps coming back. Of course it does, because you are not taking your thoughts captive. If you think the same, you will stay the same.

The spiritual warfare Paul was fighting looked quite different than what we think we're fighting today. Quit thinking that the realm of darkness is so powerful. If you think on demons you are going to get more demons. If you think they can enter you at will, they can. Light is more powerful than darkness. When you turn on a light switch, do you have any thoughts that the room will stay dark? Can the dark room put up a struggle? How quickly does the dark vanish, does it take ten years? Believe correctly, expect, and you will see the substance. We as believer's are to be casting demons out of unbelievers, not struggling with demons ourselves. Think there is a struggle then there will be.

PHILIPPIANS 4:8 (KJV)
Finally, brethren, whatsoever things are true,
whatsoever things are honest, whatsoever things
are just, whatsoever things are pure, whatsoever
things are lovely, whatsoever things are of good report; if there be any
virtue, and if there be any praise, think on these things.

COLOSSIANS 3:2 (KJV)
Set your affection on the things above
not on things on the earth.

Jesus had so much authority that the devils had to ask permission, if they could go into the pigs. Personally, I think Jesus was hungry and wanted some deviled ham! I'm joking lighten up! We have greater authority now than He did then because now we are post cross.

MATTHEW 28:18 (KJV)
And Jesus came and spake unto them
saying, All power is given unto me
in heaven and in earth.

LUKE 10:19 (KJV)
Behold, I give unto you power to tread
on serpents and scorpions, and over
all the power of the enemy: and nothing
shall by any means hurt you.

Quit thinking on all the wrong things, start renewing your mind to the mind of Christ, then we shall see changes in ourselves, others and the world. We allow the conquered realm of darkness to exalt itself over the authority of Christ. Quit feeling helpless and powerless. We are more than conquerors so start acting like it!

15 HOLY SPIRIT: DOOR UNLOCKED

We've covered a lot of topics and my goal was to provide a streamlined approach to healing. It is really quite simple when we truly understand God's nature and all that has been accomplished. The only struggle would be in breaking through old patterns that we have believed for so long. The fight comes when we look at the tragedies of life and think that life has to be this way. Our loving Father knew this; He knew there would be many misperceptions and that is why He sent Himself to reside in us. We have the fullness of Himself, The Father and Son, Jesus Christ within us as well as the Holy Spirit.

There are things that I've left out, for the sake of simplicity. The topics that I have covered, could each one be a separate book. I thank God that He has given you His Holy Spirit to teach and guide you into all truth. He will lightly tug at your heart and gently nudge you along to the spots that apply directly to you. At times, He may even slap you silly, with laughter! Last night, I was in the kitchen roasting my coffee beans, praising and worshipping Him and I felt such an overwhelming joy come over me. I love when that happens, prior to that I had been thinking about how, when and where to end this book. He nudged me, with the response, "End it with me".

My journey with the Holy Spirit, while seemingly a short five years, has been a lifetime of doing my best to avoid, run, and deny His existence. On the day of Pentecost, He was poured out onto all flesh. The question is will we listen to Him? Throughout the journey of my healing, He was speaking.

He was trying to show me, His Love, and His Healing. It wasn't until, I finally responded that indeed, I was Healed. Then over a period of a year and half, He guided me back through that journey to show me where His hand had been all along. This book has been what He's shown me, not the full extent yet; but a glimpse into it, so that you too are healed. Most of what is here, I've individually shared with those I minister to, however, in book form there is an organization involved that is better than words for some people. In this last chapter, I do want to share some things about His Holy Spirit and what I've learned about Him.

1 CORINTHIANS 6:17 (KJV)
BUT HE THAT IS JOINED UNTO THE LORD
IS ONE SPIRIT.

This scripture is relating to corporately and individually, that we were all made in His image. We come from Him. In Christ, we are made one spirit with Him again. Therefore, the bulk of our true communication comes as if it were first person. As if we're communicating with our self. We are His temple, He resides in us so He communicates with us in that way. His language to us varies, most often with me, it's not in complete thoughts but tones. It isn't even with words, more often than not. Words, are our means of communication not His. He doesn't change my personality, but does refine it. We are one spirit with Him.

Like my experience last night, He did not verbally, in loud voice tell me. He didn't even verbalize it in my thoughts, I just knew. Then today, as I was writing, He gently nudged me again. Often we miss hearing from Him because we are looking for thoughts or words. In this same way, while we are on our journey in the ministry of Christ, there are numbers of ways, He shows us how to minster. He will lead us in what the person in front of us needs; whether it be a word of knowledge, a prophetic word meant to encourage, motivate, build up, or gently correct, or a healing. He supplies it all. At the same time, He will do things to encourage us. Especially early on with praying for the sick, Holy Spirit will give us certain physical sensations, such as extreme heat in our hands or extreme cold. Many people use this manifestation to choose who to minister to or when. That's wrong; it is meant for us, to raise our expectation for other people.

Some ministers have become ensnared wrongly thinking it is validation that they alone are "anointed", or they won't minister unless they feel the physical manifestation. He simply uses the physical to lead us into the spiritual. There is a time when we need that, but don't become reliant upon those things. The first two months of my journey in praying for the sick, I would feel it every time. Then it got to the point where I didn't need it anymore. I know healing is always available, so I no longer need it, this is a sign of maturing. Oftentimes, Holy Spirit will manifest those physical things in the other person. That is awesome! That happens for that person's sake, so they can recognize what is happening. Once again, this isn't a validation of how great we are, just the same way a healing isn't a validation that the one praying for the other person is living a sanctified lifestyle, or even that he has the correct theology any more than electricity working in a home means the home owners are pure or holy. Healing is already provided for us, therefore it isn't a confirmation of us.

Maintaining a healing is easy when we have the right viewpoint. Nothing can take it away from us, unless we think that something can. I've been through that as well. There were three times the symptoms came back; I was completely paralyzed again, but I wasn't accepting it, and didn't! There was nothing that was putting me back in that wheelchair. You have to get that same backbone. If pain, comes, don't think that it has a right to stay. Don't think, "well I'm not healed." People will say, that you must always be on the lookout because the devil will try to put sickness back on you and you'll have to continue to fight for your healing. NO, we just need to have a continual relationship with Holy Spirit, to grow and mature into knowing His true nature of love. I don't fall into unbelief; the devil doesn't even have a kingdom anymore, he's defeated.

When we hear a teaching, look for confirmation from Holy Spirit, He is our educator. Seek the Kingdom of God for yourself, seek to understand His love for yourself. Speak to Him, hear His answer. Most of what I've learned has been from personal study of scriptures and learning how to hear from the Holy Spirit. We can all do this, I'm not "special". I am more than happy to impart what I've walked out and learned from the Holy Spirit. At some point you need to rely on Holy Spirit in you. God's Word gets us started, teachings from men can motivate us, testimonies can encourage us; but without an intimate relationship with the Father and Jesus all the knowledge in the world means nothing. The Pharisees had the book knowledge, yet there was no relationship. Therefore they had no (judgment) discernment, mercy or faith. Jesus told them, these were the weightier matters.

Have a conversation, and it doesn't have to be with words, but start there and then grow and mature In Christ. Speak in tongues, it edifies, beautifies and builds up your inner man. What's in the inner man flows out, so if your inner man is pure, then what flows out will be pure, healthy and vibrant.

Living a supernatural lifestyle, doesn't have to be freaky. I can and do act like myself, yet see the supernatural every day. There are many today who walk in freakiness. They are really walking in what they perceive to be walking "in the spirit", which in and of itself is walking by their physical senses. Walking in the spirit is simply walking in our true nature as believers in love. God's true nature is love. Let the Holy Spirit flow out of you, not out of what you perceive yourself to be. He will define and refine you and it isn't freaky. Well, my pot of coffee is done, and I've got things to do "in the natural", by the way I hate that saying. I gotta mow the yard!

Be blessed,
Be healed,
Be a blessing.

ABOUT THE AUTHOR

Tony Myers is author of the book "The Lord Jesus Healed Me". He lives in Virginia; with his precious wife Deb, and all their four legged family members. A former atheist, who was healed from Lou Gehrig's disease. This illness left him paralyzed and dying and then he was suddenly healed by Christ.

Since his healing on July 4th, 2012; He has appeared as a guest on many different platforms and media. This includes radio, television, and of course the internet. Most of his time is spent on his business and ministering the Gospel of Christ to others. The planned future holds more speaking engagements and more books to come. Tony is very open to be contacted for prayer, ministry, book signings and for opportunities to preach the Gospel of Christ.

Check out his website tonybelieves.com,
Facebook @tonyjustbelieves or
email: tonyjustbelieves@gmail.com.

Be sure to read "The Lord Jesus Healed Me", also by Tony.

Before you close the book, please do an Amazon Review, thanks!

83022606R00064

Made in the USA
San Bernardino, CA
20 July 2018